KW-334-512

Guidelines

VOL 25 / PART 3   September–December 2009

Edited by **Jeremy Duff and Katharine Dell**

Suggestions for using *Guidelines*

Set aside a regular time and place, if possible, when you can read and pray undisturbed. Before you begin, take time to be still and, if you find it helpful, use the BRF prayer.

In *Guidelines*, the introductory section provides context for the passages or themes to be studied, while the units of comment can be used daily, weekly, or whatever best fits your timetable. You will need a Bible (more than one if you want to compare different translations) as Bible passages are not included. At the end of each week is a 'Guidelines' section, offering further thoughts about, or practical application of what you have been studying.

You may find it helpful to keep a journal to record your thoughts about your study, or to note items for prayer. Another way of using *Guidelines* is to meet with others to discuss the material, either regularly or occasionally.

Occasionally, you may read something in *Guidelines* that you find particularly challenging, even uncomfortable. This is inevitable in a series of notes which draws on a wide spectrum of contributors, and doesn't believe in ducking difficult issues. Indeed, we believe that *Guidelines* readers much prefer thought-provoking material to a bland diet that only confirms what they already think.

If you do disagree with a contributor, you may find it helpful to go through these three steps. First, think about why you feel uncomfortable. Perhaps this is an idea that is new to you, or you are not happy at the way something has been expressed. Or there may be something more substantial—you may feel that the writer is guilty of sweeping generalization, factual error, theological or ethical misjudgment. Second, pray that God would use this disagreement to teach you more about his word and about yourself. Third, think about what you will do as a result of the disagreement. You might resolve to find out more about the issue, or write to the contributor or the editors of *Guidelines*. After all, we aim to be 'doers of the word', not just people who hold opinions about it.

Writers in this issue

Alec Gilmore is a Baptist minister, author, lecturer and Senior Research Fellow at the International Baptist Theological Seminary, Prague. His most recent book is A *Concise Dictionary of Bible Origins and Interpretation* (T&T Clark/Continuum, 2006).

Jeremy Duff is Director of Lifelong Learning in Liverpool Diocese and Canon at Liverpool Cathedral, as well as being the New Testament Editor for *Guidelines*. His latest book, *Meeting Jesus: Human Responses to a Yearning God*, was published by SPCK in 2006.

Grace Emmerson was for many years involved in Old Testament teaching in the University of Birmingham and in the Open Theological College. One of her main interests is the teaching of Hebrew and the enthusiasm it generates for biblical study. She is the author of *Nahum to Malachi* in BRF's *People's Bible Commentary* series.

Hannah Lewis is a priest in the Church of England and currently works as Team Leader for work among Deaf people in Liverpool diocese. She has been Deaf since childhood, is fluent in BSL and has been involved in the Deaf church in a variety of capacities since 1997.

Katharine Dell is Senior Lecturer in the Faculty of Divinity at Cambridge University and Director of Studies in Theology at St Catharine's College. She is also the Old Testament Editor for *Guidelines*, and the author of *Job* in BRF's *People's Bible Commentary* series.

Rob Merchant is Principal Lecturer in Spirituality and Health at Staffordshire University. He is ordained in the Church of England and supports two parishes in Cheltenham. He is also the author of *Pioneering the Third Age: The Church in an Ageing Population* (Paternoster, 2003).

Paula Gooder teaches Biblical studies, both Old and New Testament, at the Queen's Ecumenical Theological Foundation, Birmingham, as well as working freelance as a biblical studies writer and lecturer. She is the author of *Hosea to Micah* in BRF's *People's Bible Commentary* series.

David Spriggs is a Baptist Minister, working for Bible Society as Consultant for Bible and Church. He also provides oversight in his church in the absence of a ministry leader. He continues to be amazed at scripture's potency to shape our lives as we allow the Holy Spirit to work in us.

·············· Further BRF reading for this issue ··············

For more in-depth coverage of some of the passages in these
Bible reading notes, we recommend the following titles:

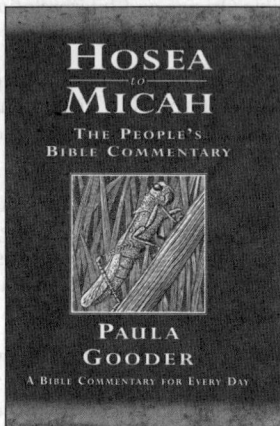

HOSEA to MICAH

THE PEOPLE'S BIBLE COMMENTARY

PAULA GOODER

A BIBLE COMMENTARY FOR EVERY DAY

978 1 84101 245 2, £8.99

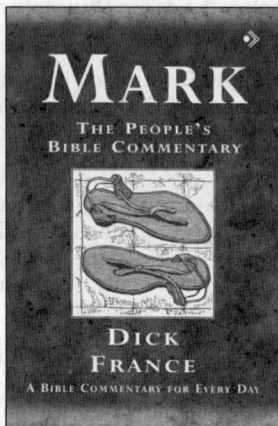

MARK

THE PEOPLE'S BIBLE COMMENTARY

DICK FRANCE

A BIBLE COMMENTARY FOR EVERY DAY

978 1 84101 046 5, £8.99

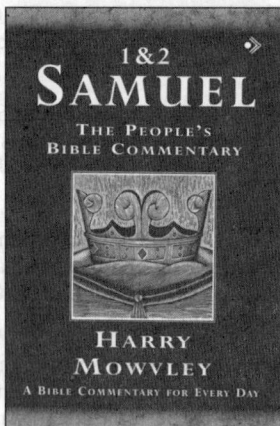

1 & 2 SAMUEL

THE PEOPLE'S BIBLE COMMENTARY

HARRY MOWVLEY

A BIBLE COMMENTARY FOR EVERY DAY

978 1 84101 030 4, £7.99

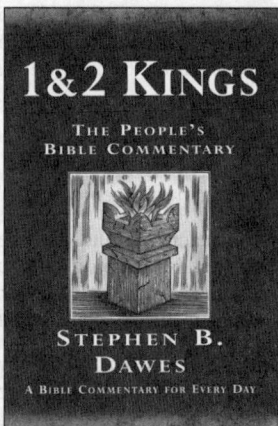

1 & 2 KINGS

THE PEOPLE'S BIBLE COMMENTARY

STEPHEN B. DAWES

A BIBLE COMMENTARY FOR EVERY DAY

978 1 84101 118 9, £7.99

The Editors write...

In this issue we continue our journey through the 'former prophets', featuring 2 Samuel by Grace Emmerson and 2 Kings from Paula Gooder, both writers familiar to *Guidelines* readers. These are important books of the history of the monarchic period but they are also theologically rich and formative for the Israelite faith as it comes to literary expression.

We also have contributions in this issue from David Spriggs on Joel and Alec Gilmore on Jonah. These minor prophets both have short but important messages that can usefully be 'reread' afresh for today.

In the New Testament we have the second part of our study of Mark's Gospel, in which Jeremy Duff helps us engage with the themes of 'the law', 'miracles' and 'the death of Jesus'. Luke will be our Gospel for 2010. Therefore our Christmas readings this year are taken from Luke's Gospel; we will continue from where we leave off in the next edition. Luke's Christmas story is full of expectation and fulfilment as we see God's action going beyond what was expected.

We have three challenging thematic pieces in this edition. Hannah Lewis, herself Deaf and a priest in the Church of England, writes for us on Deaf theology, unveiling for us the rich perspective that the Deaf bring to the Bible. Katharine Dell has written on 'The dark side of God', drawing out Old Testament texts that present an unusual view of God as making excessive demands on his servants, appearing to act capriciously or being prepared to change his mind when challenged. Finally, in a very open, honest and personal set of notes called 'Walking the psalms', Rob Merchant shares with us his own journey of mental health.

This is Katharine Dell's last edition as commissioning editor. She writes: 'As outgoing editor, I would like to thank all those at BRF who have made it an enjoyable eight years as editor, especially Richard Fisher, Naomi Starkey and Lisa Cherrett. I would like to thank John Parr and Jeremy Duff who have been co-editors during the period. Especial thanks, of course, go to you the readers for your many letters and encouraging remarks and to those contributors who have had their arms twisted by me for some wonderful contributions over the years. And my chief hope is that *Guidelines* continues to go from strength to strength in the future.'

The BRF Prayer

Almighty God,
you have taught us that your word is a lamp for our
feet and a light for our path. Help us, and all who
prayerfully read your word, to deepen our
fellowship with each other through your love. And
in so doing may we come to know you more fully,
love you more truly, and follow more faithfully in
the steps of your son Jesus Christ, who lives and
reigns with you and the Holy Spirit,
one God for evermore. Amen.

A Prayer for Remembrance

Heavenly Father, we commit ourselves to work in
penitence and faith for reconciliation between the
nations, that all people may, together, live in
freedom, justice and peace. We pray for all who in
bereavement, disability and pain continue to suffer
the consequences of fighting and terror. We
remember with thanksgiving and sorrow those
whose lives, in world wars and conflicts past and
present, have been given and taken away.

FROM AN ORDER OF SERVICE FOR REMEMBRANCE SUNDAY,
CHURCHES TOGETHER IN BRITAIN AND IRELAND 2005

JONAH FOR TODAY

Jonah is not history, nor is it based on history, and it probably was never intended to be taken literally. Described by one scholar (Meik Gerhards) as 'a didactic novelette', it raises deep and sensitive issues about monotheism, race and culture in the context of a small nation with a large ego, surrounded and outplayed by many bigger fish, which suddenly finds itself face-to-face with people whose understanding of God and experience of faith is totally different from theirs.

The book is usually dated in the fourth century BC (or a little later), when Jews who had been living in Babylon for two or three generations started to return. Some were of a generation which had never known Jerusalem. Some may have been Babylonians (foreigners) taking the opportunity to make a new life in a new world. Some who had never left Jerusalem were not enamoured of the newcomers and resented their tendency to arrive as if they owned the place, causing hurt and unrest among those who had been left behind, who felt that they had carried many of the burdens.

Ezra and Nehemiah, two of the returnees, were trying to rebuild life as it once was (or as they thought it once was), whereas some returnees found it all very different from what they remembered and were not sure they wanted to abandon everything they had left behind. In all the tensions, the faith of Judaism was being shaken to the core as it wrestled with the problem of one faith and one God coming sharply into contact with alternatives that showed no sign of going away.

Four different attitudes are reflected by the principal characters in the drama: Jonah, the sailors, the Ninevites, and God. We need to read, reflect and pray to see whether we find ourselves in the story and, if so, where exactly and whether we are content with what we see.

The notes are based on the New Revised Standard Version of the Bible.

1 Jonah

Jonah 1:1–6

Whether you take this 'call' literally or whether you think of it as one of those urges we all get from time to time, telling us there is something we must do, it must have been one of the most unbelievable ever heard or felt. Nineveh's reputation didn't bear thinking about, and Jonah's reaction was vehement. He had nothing in common with those people; he wouldn't touch them with a barge pole. If he'd told his friends what was being proposed, they would have questioned his sanity. Try to reason with people like the Ninevites and you are on a hiding to nothing. Daniel's den of lions would be a holiday in comparison, and if Jonah escaped with his life he would feel scarred and contaminated for ever.

Unfortunately the urge won't go away. There is only one thing to do: pack his bag, get as far away as he can in the opposite direction, and retire.

There are two questions to explore. First, since the call of God (or the urge) rarely comes from nowhere, where did this call come from? Of the reputation of the Ninevites, Jonah knew plenty, but what did he really know about the people? Had he met any face-to-face or had he been listening to the gossip, 'reading the tabloids' and believing without question what everybody wanted to hear? Were the Ninevites all the same, and what did he expect to achieve simply by 'crying out against' them (v. 2)?

Second, even if everything he'd heard was true, why was he so uptight about it? Was there something he knew he had to come to terms with and could not face? Or was 'Nineveh' a world that, deep down, fascinated him and frightened him at the same time? Perhaps it was somewhere he had always wanted to go and been told that he mustn't. He might even have tried once and got his fingers burnt.

If you have ever been in a similar situation, you will not find it difficult to identify with Jonah. If not, you probably know someone who has been. Think of it as your 'Nineveh moment'. Use your imagination to make the story your own. Work out what you felt and how you handled the same sort of issues.

2 The sailors

The trouble with God's urges is that you can't escape them. Run away and you take them with you. God comes again, this time in the form of an enormous storm—at sea, of all places. Jonah suddenly finds himself once again (literally and metaphorically) in deep waters. He can neither answer the call nor escape it. In his attempt to avoid those dreadful people (the pagans, the heathen, the unbelievers), he now finds himself confronted by a captain and a crew who (whatever else they are) are not part of the faithful. They want to know who he is and what he thinks he is doing. It's his new 'Nineveh moment'.

This is a story of what happens when a person with a very strong sense of calling comes into close proximity with a group of people from another faith and they find themselves facing a common problem in a time of crisis. Think again about your own Nineveh moment and see if you can identify the sailors in it. Compare these two reactions.

The sailors, far from running away, first cry to *their* god for help and then set about doing what is practical and possible. Next, they involve their nearest contact (Jonah), investigate possible causes and look for reasons and solutions, including the supernatural: this thing might be 'of God' (vv. 10, 14). They then struggle to the limits of their ability. They display a basic humanitarianism, even refusing to ditch Jonah when he presents himself as the cause of the storm and actually invites them to throw him overboard. They display qualities of wisdom, selflessness, piety and faithfulness, which Jonah appears unable to recognise or emulate; they remain people whose faith and way of life he seems totally unable to appreciate. To the sailors, the problem seems to be an oddball they have unfortunately encountered on the sea of life.

Jonah, on the other hand, has little positive to offer. Obsessed with himself, he has scant regard for those who refuse to see everything through his eyes. Even in a time of deep distress, which he is sharing with the sailors, he fails to demonstrate the quality of life that might draw them to God.

Which of these two reactions would you expect to find yourself demonstrating? Which reaction would you like others to see in you?

3 Jonah and the fish

The description of these verses as 'A psalm of thanksgiving' is a recent misnomer and best ignored. On the surface, it might appear that Jonah's experience in the belly of the fish concentrated his mind and inspired a brief act of repentance which would enable God to give him a second chance, but the future tense (v. 9) suggests that his prayer is much more like a plea for deliverance, if not a bit of unadulterated bargaining. The experience has done nothing to allay this man's turmoil, anger and arrogance.

This is hardly surprising. When we're sure that we are right, and are driven into a tight corner, our prejudices are usually fortified, our worst fears realised and our arrogance intensified. This seems to have happened to Jonah.

Trevor Dennis spells out the man's self-centredness. Count the number of times he uses 'I' and 'me'. Forgetting that he actually asked to be dumped into the sea, he now vents his anger on God (v. 3). Sometimes he seems to be whistling in the dark (v. 6) but, as arrogance breeds self-confidence, platitudes flow like water. Jonah knows he is right, knows he will be vindicated, and the psalm ends as he unfolds his plans for the future. The final line is almost, 'Deliver me... or else.' Dennis says that the psalm made God sick: no wonder the fish did what he did.

But could this psalm be a fair reflection of what many of us would feel (indeed, have felt) in similar circumstances? Jonah is the epitome of those people in every age, ethnic group and religion for whom everything is black and white and who find no difficulty in dividing the world into two—those who see it their way and know their God, and those who don't.

How different is the reaction of the sailors—possibly closer to the attitude of some of Jonah's contemporaries within Judaism. The sailors have no doubt who they believe in and pray to (1:5) but seem able to accommodate different gods (or expressions of God) for different peoples. They understand that Yahweh is the God of Israel. In company with Jonah, they can even pray to him (1:14). Compare the respect they show to Jonah's God with the respect he shows to the gods of other nations (as reflected in his attitude to the people of Nineveh). Contrast their turning to God with Jonah's running away from him. Which do we want to live with?

4 The people of Nineveh

Jonah 3

Of the people of Nineveh we know very little, except that when Jonah is thought to have been written (in the fourth century BC or even later) the city was a pale shadow of its former glory. As the last city of the Assyrian empire, however, destroyed in 612BC, its reputation as the scourge of the Middle East lived on.

Meik Gerhards suggests that, for Israel, Nineveh stood for all the superpowers (Egypt, Babylon, Persia) in their history. Dennis describes it as an icon of everything evil in the ancient world, whose armies were masters of psychological warfare, the terrorists of the Middle East, convinced of their own invincibility.

To keep the story alive for today, work out where we find the 'Ninevites' popping up in our psyche. Is this how many parts of the Commonwealth still feel about the British Empire? How the USA still feels about the Soviet bloc? Or how Western Europe feels about Nazism? We must not deny past horrors, but at times we all find it difficult to accept that our impression of others is an image of the past that bears little relation to the present.

The city of Nineveh was very different from the city described here, and the extreme detail makes it clear that we are now in the realm of storyland. It was no more than three square miles in area, its walls measured less than eight miles in circumference, there is no evidence that it ever had a king, and a population of 120,000 (4:11) seems somewhat overstated. Though very different from what it was in its seventh-century heyday, the ghost from the past still walks and people tremble.

What Jonah failed to appreciate was the gap between the Ninevites' reputation, which he had been brought up on (the way he saw them), and the reality (the way God saw them). Starting with a picture of a loving God, the storyteller wants to present a merciful God, challenging such presuppositions and prejudices. Why? Possibly because, in Jonah's world, truth, mercy, understanding and an acceptance of those who were different were hard to come by. In God's world, however, Jonah's fears and prejudices were of much less significance, as the issues called for a quite different approach.

5 The bush: encounter with God

As in all short stories, there are things here that we are not told: they are left to our imagination. Compare what Jonah 'heard' in 1:2 with what he 'heard' in 3:2. Mention of their 'wickedness' has gone and he has to wait for further instructions. Imagination then raises other questions. Had Jonah perhaps misheard—or heard but misunderstood? Had he received a call from God or was Jonah just attributing to God some of his own ill feelings? It sounds as if he sensed a call from God to go and do something that, from the start, could never work (v. 2).

Certainly this arrogant customer is both angry and miserable—angry at the call, angry inside the fish, angry when he shouts at the people of Nineveh, angry with God for being generous, angry with his own success, and presumably angry with himself for ever getting involved. He knew all along what would happen—so he sits in a corner and sulks.

Temporary respite comes when, despite being the victim of Jonah's wrath, the God who is generous with the people of Nineveh is equally generous to Jonah, giving him the protection of the bush. Jonah is delighted: it ministers to his self-centredness; perhaps he feels that it confirms his judgment that God is with him. But the satisfaction is temporary. Within 24 hours the bush has gone, the heat is on and Jonah is back where he started.

By this stage, we might have thought that even Jonah would begin to ask questions and even take a look at himself. But no. For Jonah, nothing has changed. How could his God, who had always had a special relationship with his people, and whom they had loved and served for more years than they could count, suddenly show favour to a crew as dreadful as those people in Nineveh? It made no sense. Was everybody now to be on the same level? Were unbelievers to be treated as mercifully as those who had always remained faithful? And if they were, what message was this going to send out to all the other heathen, pagans and infidels? No—Jonah is still sure he is right. He would rather die than ask the question.

6 God and the bush

Jonah 4:9–11

The story that began with a challenge ends with a question. It is a question that forces an arrogant and angry man to look at himself. It is not a question about his faith, what he was asked to do, why he didn't (or couldn't) do it, or why he felt as he did about the people of Nineveh. Nor is it the beginning of a lecture on what he ought to do, complete with detailed instructions as to what God requires. In moments of such extreme arrogance and anger, Jonah, like the rest of us, has to answer a different question that God is asking: 'Is it right for you to feel like this?'

Only when it is clear that Jonah is still not talking does the Almighty feel the need to spell it out—and the word of God is very simple. He asks Jonah to see it from his point of view, and, to help Jonah get there, invites him to look for the answer in his own experience. If Jonah knows what it feels like to lose something very precious (like the bush) when he did nothing to put it there in the first place, can he not imagine how God feels when he sees a whole city—which he has created and in which he has invested so much—proving unresponsive to his overtures. Can Jonah not begin to understand what it feels like when there is, at last, a sign of a positive response?

And there the story ends. We are not told whether Jonah can or he can't, but now it is no longer a story about Jonah and the people of Nineveh, and the fish fades into insignificance. It is a story about us.

First, clarify your thoughts by trying to answer some simple questions. Did his encounter with God make any difference to Jonah? Did he sit down and write out a confession? Far from changing the lives of others (the Ninevites), did it really change his life, or did he continue as before? Next, see if you can write (or rewrite) your 'Nineveh moment' in the light of Jonah's experience. How different is it from the way you might have written it only a week ago?

Guidelines

- Try writing the next chapter of the Jonah story. When Jonah returned home, with whom do you think he shared this experience? How do you think he might have told the story? What do you think his hearers might have said in response?
- If you belong to group, try a little role-play with Jonah, a couple of sailors, a Ninevite reflecting on the fact that his city is no longer the jewel in the crown of the Assyrian empire, and the voice of God.
- Initiate discussion among friends on the similarities between Jonah, representing the hardliners in the Jewish community in the fourth century BC, and people with similar views in your own community today. See if you can identify the different characters.

FURTHER READING

Trevor Dennis, *Lo and Behold! The Power of Old Testament Storytelling*, SPCK, 1991 (pp. 133–55).

Trevor Dennis, *The Book of Books: The Bible Retold*, Lion, 2003 (pp. 252–61).

Meik Gerhards, 'Studien zum Jonabuch' (Biblische-theologische Studen 78), Neukirchener Verlag, 2006.

Jonathan Magonet, *A Rabbi Reads the Bible*, SCM, revised edition 2004 (pp. 94–96, 115, 155–56).

Charles M. Laymon (ed.), *The Interpreter's One-Volume Commentary on the Bible*, Abingdon Press, 1971.

MARCAN THEMES (PART 2)

This is the second part of our study of themes in Mark's Gospel. As explained in the last edition, this extended thematic look at a Gospel is a one-off: from January 2010 we will return to our pattern of studying a Gospel passage by passage. Nevertheless, I hope that encountering Mark's Gospel in this alternative, thematic fashion will shed new light on familiar Gospel stories, and so help us to grow in discipleship and be doers as well as hearers of the word.

In the last edition we looked at discipleship, parables and the question 'Who is Jesus?' This time we consider the Law, miracles and the death of Jesus. There are, of course, other themes that could have been chosen, but I believe that together these get us to the heart of Mark's message about Jesus.

Mark's Gospel is generally regarded as being the first Gospel committed to writing, probably in the 60s AD. Most scholars believe that it inspired the whole idea of 'a Gospel' as a written text, and was known and used by Matthew and Luke and perhaps John. It is traditionally associated with Peter and there is good reason to believe that this association is reliable. Mark himself is an unknown character from the early Church, with no claim to be an apostle or an eyewitness: the fact that the Gospel gained such widespread recognition suggests that it was generally known that someone of great authority, such as Peter, lay behind it.

Quotations in these notes have been taken from the New Revised Standard Version of the Bible.

Miracles

1 Authority and power

Mark 1:21–34

Jesus' ministry begins with the proclamation that the kingdom of God is near (1:15). This is followed by two stories which flag up much that will follow in the Gospel—first, the calling of the disciples, explored in the last edition in the theme of discipleship; then the healing, teaching and the casting out of demons, presented as part of a single activity.

The overriding tone of this passage is that Jesus is good news for the people. We might notice that the healings happen on the sabbath (v. 21) and see this as potentially bringing conflict, but there is no real note of that here. Jesus' activity is simply good news. Amazing, yes, and the crowds gather (vv. 32–34), but welcome.

There are many details in this passage that repay further thought. Notice the healing of Simon's mother-in-law: Simon's discipleship, while seeming to be at the expense of his previous life, actually brought good to those around him. (Her immediately waiting on them might sound harsh to our ears, but seems to be the proof of success and re-entry into normal society that we find after almost all of Jesus' healings.) We will look at the idea of casting out demons in the next reading; for now, note that it was seen as proof that God's power was at work for the people's good. The question of why the demons were not allowed to speak intrigues us all (we discussed it in greater depth in the last edition): perhaps demons are not worthy revealers of Jesus' identity; perhaps powerful miracles do not actually reveal Jesus' true nature.

Jesus is said to teach with authority. Presumably this was a matter of his style—perhaps because he gave his own judgments rather than just articulating an extensive tradition. Scholars think that this is what the 'teaching of the law' did (see 7:5), although the evidence is patchy. Fundamental to this sense of authority, however, is the fact that Jesus didn't just speak but also acted to bring good and release from evil. Jesus did not just proclaim good news; he brought it. Indeed, he was it.

This relates directly to our context. Particularly now, in our postmodern and somewhat cynical world, talk is cheap, but action and integrity between words and deeds bring respect. We know that this is how we assess others, whether friends or politicians: 'Is it all just talk?' But this is also, rightly, how our discipleship and the church itself is judged. Are we just talk? Do we just proclaim good news or do we bring it? Is our church good news in our community?

2 The prince of demons

Mark 3:20–30

Demons are at the heart of Mark's Gospel. This is an inconvenient embarrassment for many of us in the Western world today. At best, we don't think of demons at all; at worst, we associate talk of exorcisms and demons with unpleasant and definitely non-Christian groupings. But we can't avoid the fact that conflict with demons is a key element in the presentation of Jesus. Indeed, as we have seen, his first miracle was the casting out of a demon, not a healing, and the disciples were sent out to preach and cast out demons (no mention of healing: see 3:13–15).

What can we say? First, the talk of demons reminds us that the world of the Gospels is not our world. As we see ourselves in the actions of the disciples, we can feel that the distance between 'then' and 'now' shrinks to nothing, but the demons remind us that cultures and worldviews shape profoundly how we understand what we experience. We may prefer our way of understanding the world but we need humility when encountering others', whether separated from us by time or space. Often, Western academics have declared that the situations described in such passages as being caused by demons were 'actually' mental illness. There may be some truth in this, but we also need to be honest and admit that this is simply an assertion that *as a matter of principle* everything that the Gospel writers put in one category (demons) must fit into a certain one of ours (mental illness).

If we look past our understandable nervousness about the language of demons, we can see the point that everyone, even Jesus' enemies, recognised that in his presence evil was being overturned. The language of 'a kingdom divided' immediately reminds us of the 'kingdom of God' that Jesus proclaimed (1:15). Jesus' driving out of the demons is part of the destruction of powers opposed to God and the establishment of God's reign. (This is made explicit in Matthew's and Luke's versions of this story: Matthew 12:28 and Luke 11:20; for the language of transfer between two kingdoms, see also Colossians 1:13.)

When we think about our world, we recognise that there is much that oppresses people and destroys life, which cannot simply be seen as the actions of individual people—institutions, cultures, history and expectations. These too must be rolled back if God's kingdom is to be manifested. Jesus did this, and people experienced it as truly miraculous. He instructed his disciples to do the same.

3 The feeding of the five thousand

Mark 6:30–44

This miracle is presented in such a simple and understated manner, and yet it seems astonishing. Many feel that they can comprehend miraculous healing in some sense, but this feeding seems beyond explanation. (Some might suggest that what actually happened was everyone shared their packed lunches, but that is not the story we are given here. I fail to see any justification for rewriting the story to suit ourselves.)

Provision is the key point, though, not the display of miraculous power. We begin with Jesus making provision for his apostles. They may have been filled with God's power to work wonders (6:7–13), yet they still had natural human needs. It is easy for those caught up in God's purposes to neglect the reality of their own needs, particularly for rest and emotional fulfilment.

Then Jesus provides for the crowd. The description of them as 'sheep without a shepherd' (v. 34) is full of significance, for Ezekiel 34 talks of God's people being like sheep with nobody to care for them (for example, v. 6). The appointed shepherds (the teachers of the law, Pharisees and temple authorities) have misused and neglected their position, with the result that God himself comes to shepherd them and provide for them. Thus the phrase contains an implicit criticism of the 'appointed shepherds'. It also suggests that God was acting in Jesus.

The disciples think that Jesus' response to the crowd will be limited to teaching (vv. 34–36) but, as we have seen, Jesus' teaching goes along with action, so he provides for the crowd's physical needs. Indeed, since he provides for them through the disciples, it is almost as if he is appointing new shepherds to replace the old, corrupt ones. The result is overflowing provision (vv. 42–43).

Another set of connections is commonly seen in this story, and is developed in John 6. First, there is a connection with the Passover (John 6:4). Mark's detail that the grass was green (v. 39) would fit with this, given that Passover is celebrated in the spring. Second, the act of feeding the masses in a 'deserted place' (v. 35) suggests God's provision of manna during the exodus (John 6:31–33). Finally, the sequence of taking, giving thanks, breaking and giving (v. 41) matches the Eucharist (Mark 14:22; John 6:48–58). It seems reasonable to conclude that the early Christians, looking back on this miraculous feeding, saw these connections—Jesus feeding the people at the new Passover of the Eucharist.

Undoubtedly this feeding is miraculous, but that doesn't seem to be the point. What matters is God's provision for the crowds, provision that the disciples are called to facilitate. Who are the 'sheep without a shepherd' today, and what is our response to them?

4 The healing of a deaf and dumb man

Mark 7:31–37

Here we have a healing story that fits the general pattern for such miracles—although each always has its own particular features. Here we note that there is no expression of faith or desire to be healed by the man himself, just by 'some people' (v. 32, NIV). Of course, we might say that because of his disability they had to speak for him, but we have to be careful not to squash all such stories into a fixed form in which 'faith' is a requirement for healing. This account does not mention faith; indeed, perhaps there is encouragement here for us to act in support of, and even on behalf of, those who cannot help themselves, such as the very young, the very old and those who are physically or mentally very sick.

Immediately, though, we also face the complication of the paternalism that this passage could imply towards deaf and dumb people. This is discussed in more depth elsewhere in this issue of *Guidelines*, but it is worth remembering the particular, complex resonances of this passage for an important segment of our population.

Jesus' actions are intriguing. If the healing took place at Jesus' word, as is normally the case and seems to be implied here, what was the point of the touching? We will never know. More interesting, perhaps, is why Mark has preserved this detail, as well as the precise Aramaic word used by Jesus, which would have meant nothing to Mark's readers. It certainly gives a vividness and sense of mystery to the account. The most obvious and credible explanation is that this particular healing caused a huge impression on those who saw it.

Indeed, that is the sense given in verses 36–37: it was seen as a profound miracle. Partly, this is simply because it was amazing. The wording in the final verse points to a deeper reason, however. At least, Matthew (11:5) and Luke (7:22) see it that way, understanding this kind of healing as being a 'sign of the Messiah'. Thus, 'he has done everything well' (v. 37) may not mean just 'He has brought good to this man' but also 'He is behaving as the Messiah should.'

Jesus, though, seems not to have wanted this kind of praise. He commands silence again. Soon, on the road to Caesarea Philippi, after the healing of a blind man, the title of Messiah is put to Jesus. His response is lukewarm at best (8:29–30). We might be amazed at and even long for 'miracles', but for Jesus they were not central to his identity.

5 I believe; help my unbelief

Mark 9:14–29

This account brings to the forefront the question of faith. It has already been mentioned earlier—the women with haemorrhaging was told, 'Your faith has made you well' (5:34)—but in other healings faith has not been mentioned explicitly (for example, 1:39–45) and in some it is the faith of others, not the sick person, that is mentioned (for example, 2:5).

The issue is raised first by Jesus' declaration, 'You faithless generation, how much longer must I be among you?' (v. 19). It is not clear, however, whose lack of faith is being criticised. Is it the disciples'? In the previous chapter the disciples have been called hard-hearted (8:17) and Peter 'Satan' (v. 33). Did their lack of faith mean that they could not drive out the spirit (9:18)? Or is the criticism directed at the boy and his father? Perhaps we are mistaken to try to connect the lack of faith to the failure of the exorcism: maybe Jesus' outburst is a more generalised comment on his generation (compare his outbursts about Capernaum and Jerusalem in Luke 10:15; 19:41–44).

Jesus' exchange with the father (vv. 21–25) has an honesty about it which is memorable and appealing. It has many similarities with the healing of the Syrophoenician woman's daughter (7:24–30). In both cases, an initial approach to Jesus meets with a cool response, which seems to be transformed by a clever, quick reply. In some ways this is troubling. Is Jesus' action dependent on clever repartee? Perhaps we should take it as a reminder of the reality of the incarnation: Jesus truly became human and so his actions were shaped by what happened around him. He was not, and is not, an emotionless robot.

The father's cry, 'I believe; help my unbelief!' expresses the deep mystery of faith. Faith itself is a gift from God (Ephesians 2:8), and yet it is also the basis on which we can relate to God. That could seem like a 'Catch 22' but this exchange proves otherwise: Jesus does not require faith, only the desire for faith.

Jesus' final comment, 'This kind can come out only through prayer', (v. 29) is intriguing. Was this a special kind of demon? Who knows? What is clear, though, is the central role of prayer and, more broadly, of reliance on God. Faith itself is reliance on God, and prayer is a vehicle for expressing that reliance and also the means by which our relationship with God, and faith itself, are built up. How do we build up our faith?

6 Blind Bartimaeus

Mark 10:46–52

This is the final healing in Mark's Gospel and, in some senses, the final 'miracle' (though still to come are the cursing of the fig tree, the tearing of the temple curtain and, of course, the resurrection). Many of the features of the story are similar to others in the Gospels—the initial approach by the one needing healing, Jesus' welcome for the person, the exchange, the healing and the proof of healing. Unusually, though, at the end the healed person travels with Jesus 'on the way'.

This points us to a key feature of the story. While it seems like a healing story, it is just as much a story of discipleship, for Bartimaeus does not just meet Jesus and ask. He has to overcome obstacles—his own blindness, but also the opposition of those around him. They amplify his physical difficulties with their attitude: surely Jesus would not be interested in someone like him. His place is to sit and receive what people choose to give him, not to cry out, demanding attention—but Bartimaeus is having none of it. Yes, he is motivated by his desire for healing, but he also shows a great faith in Jesus and confidence in Jesus' welcome of those marginalized in society, as he continues to cry out. Jesus then asks him, 'What do you want me to do for you?' (v. 51). At face value this seems a bizarre question: isn't it obvious? He wants to see!

This story provides a lens through which to look at our own discipleship. What barriers keep us away from meeting with Jesus? Most of us feel that most of the time Jesus is there but not really with us—next door, maybe, or on the other side of the crowd. But what is the barrier—issues within us? For Bartimaeus, it was his blindness (an easy metaphor for our own spiritual shortsightedness). Or is the problem really the opinions of those around us or our own fears about what people will think? Bartimaeus demonstrates singlemindedness and the need for wholehearted, urgent response to Jesus. Jesus' question continues the same theme. 'What do you want?' is a question few of us ask of ourselves. We are carried along by expectations and assumptions; life just keeps going. But what is it we want? What do we want enough to have Bartimaeus' singlemindedness and courage?

Guidelines

The word 'miracles' can easily lock us into a particular, rather tired argument. The 'believer' tries to assert that the miracles really happened and that they therefore prove that Jesus was God. The 'sceptic' says that the evidence is not sufficient, and remains sceptical about Jesus' divinity. But this argument misses the point of the 'miracles' that we have seen. They were not about demonstrating who Jesus was. Indeed, he seemed to be constantly trying to stop people drawing conclusions from them about his identity.

Instead, we find that Jesus' works of power were about bringing good news in deeds as well as words—reaching people where they needed it most, challenging oppression and providing for people. Their effect seems to be not so much about generating faith ('if only God would do something, I would believe') but about highlighting both lack of faith and faith and determination in unusual quarters (such as Bartimaeus).

If this is true, then we have no excuse. Most of us might not be able to do 'miracles' but we can bring good news in deeds as well as words, reach people where they need it most, challenge oppression, provide for people, and show singlemindedness in our discipleship with Jesus. If you took on that challenge, how would you live differently next week?

Law

1 The wrong company

Mark 2:14–20

The short account of the calling of Levi contains so much. At the heart of it lies the question of the differences in approach between Jesus and the Pharisees. While we must be careful when we turn real people (the Pharisees) into representatives of a particular way of thinking, we see in this story two different approaches to the work of God in the world.

To understand the Pharisees' complaint, we have to recognise that the 'tax collectors and sinners' (v. 16) were not the poor, or those margin-alised because of disease, age or gender. Nor, in the word 'sinners', should we see a reference to all of us. These were people who had chosen to abandon their Jewish heritage—working for the oppressive heathen occupying power or, in other ways, living with a disregard for the covenant. They were people who had chosen a life of sin, not people who happened to do things wrong. If Jesus were calling such people and telling them to change their ways, his behaviour would be acceptable, but that is not what is happening. He seems simply to be spending time with them socially (verse 16 suggests that this is not a one-off incident), relaxing with them and enjoying their company—implying publicly that

23

God is content with them and likes them. What example does this set?

Jesus' response seems straightforward—he has come to save sinners —but it begs two questions. First, that might be true, but isn't there the danger that in the process he is giving out the wrong message? Isn't he undermining standards in the community and ruining his own reputation as a holy man? Perhaps, but Jesus doesn't seem to care. Saving these people is more important than a general sense of reputation. Second, how do you 'save sinners'? Jesus' answer seems to be that it is less about preaching at them and more about living with them, less about demanding that they change and more about accepting them as they are.

The discussion of fasting (vv. 18–20) puts the issue into a wider perspective. Jesus says that he is a special person (the bridegroom) at a special time ('while he is with them… the days will come'). The normal structures of life ('fasting') do have their place, but God has sent him on a particular mission 'to call sinners'.

We now live with this tension. As Jesus' disciples we are called, surely, to have his attitude towards 'sinners', but isn't there also some place for publicly upholding standards, for supporting those who are trying to be good, not those who choose wickedness instead?

2 Lord of the sabbath

Mark 2:23–28

This passage appears to be an argument about the interpretation of the law (not the law itself). When the Pharisees claim that the disciples are doing what is 'not lawful on the sabbath' (v. 24), what they mean is that the disciples are breaking the Pharisees' interpretation of the law. The law itself simply says, 'Do not work on the Sabbath' (see Exodus 20:10), but what is 'work'? In an attempt to answer this question, to pin down what God does or does not require, the Pharisees had created further definitions, according to which the disciples were 'working' and hence breaking the law. The Pharisees had no direct power to enforce their will but did so by exactly this sort of public challenge. 'Hey, you, why are you doing that? It's wrong' from a respected community figure will normally cause self-doubt and shame in those challenged.

Jesus' response is to point to an inconsistency within the law (as recorded in the Old Testament): David took bread which only priests should eat, and fed it to his men. This can itself be seen in two ways. Firstly, we can focus on the link between Jesus, David and 'the Son of Man'. David was able to do what he did because he was David. So, too, the normal rules do not apply to Jesus. He is, after all, the 'lord of the sabbath' (v. 28), so the sabbath rules are flexible in his presence. This interpretation would gain strength from the discussion in the previous reading of 'the bridegroom', where rules seemed to be changed in Jesus' presence.

However, this is not the only possible interpretation, for in verse 27 Jesus says, 'The sabbath was made for humankind.' Thus, it seems, the point is not that Jesus was special so the rules didn't apply to him; he is making a general statement about the relationship between the law and humankind, with 'the Son of Man' meaning simply a representation of all people. The law is there to benefit people; if it is confining people, it should give way. The story about David does not demonstrate that the rules bent for David, but that the rules bent in the face of need. This interpretation gains further support from the passage following, where the key question (in respect of healing on the sabbath) is 'Is it lawful to do good or to do harm on the sabbath, to save life or to kill?' (3:4). Any rules of the sabbath are to be overruled by a general imperative to do good.

Of course we can easily see this as merely of antiquarian interest, but the same question would apply to ethical and religious principles within Christianity. How flexible should they be?

3 Religious rules

Mark 7:1–23

Notice first two details. Scribes have come down from Jerusalem (Jesus is gaining some notoriety), and the explanation in verses 3–4 suggests that Mark is writing for a non-Jewish audience.

What do we, most of us also non-Jews, make of the teaching here? It is easy to simply categorise 'all this stuff about food laws' as an example of 'Jewish tradition', and to feel self-congratulatory that Christianity has 'moved on' from such externals. Protestant Christians, particularly of 'new church', more evangelical backgrounds, often feel that they particularly have taken to heart a message here about the importance of rejecting human tradition. Jesus certainly seems to be challenging the direction in which much of Jewish religious teaching had been going in the previous couple of centuries, in which an oral tradition had been developed ('the tradition of the elders', v. 3), aimed at clarifying in detail what people must do in order to be holy ('undefiled'). This tradition was certainly not 'all about externals' but it did include attempts to define what God required in increasing detail (for example, as we saw in the previous reading, what constitutes 'work').

We should look at the case in question, however. Jesus is attacking a process (Corban: v. 11) through which a gift was dedicated to God, and insisting that the first call on someone's money should not be God but their parents, because that is what the commandment requires. So does truly following God's commandments mean less 'religion'?

The final part of the passage (vv. 14–23) certainly does seem to talk about food laws but, even here, we need to think carefully. When we look at the list of things that, according to Jesus, 'defile' a person, few if any of them relate to 'religion' in the sense of being acts done or words said relating to God. There is nothing here about worship, spirituality or prayer—how to do them or how not to. Little is specifically Christian or Jewish. What we have is a fairly straightforward presentation of a moral life, with a focus on treatment of others.

Thus, perhaps we do have a unity with Jesus' comment on the 'Corban' teaching. Jesus appears to be challenging the notion that what God requires is 'religion'—religious observance, spirituality or holiness. It is a warning for us all because it is easy for religious institutions and people to value 'religion' more than those simple but hard matters of how we treat others, which, in Jesus' words, 'come from the heart'.

4 Is divorce OK?

Mark 10:2–12

Breakdown of marriage is not new. It is certainly true that divorce itself is more of a feature of our society now than in the past, but of course it is very hard to know how that correlates to the quality of marriages.

We need to understand this passage carefully. The background is the movement within Judaism to define more precisely what was lawful and what was not. On the issue of divorce there were two camps, a more liberal and a more conservative interpretation of Moses' command. Both, however, worked on the basis that once it was clear in what circumstances it was lawful, then a man (within traditional Judaism, only a man could instigate divorce) was entitled to do it. According to this way of thinking, once we define clearly what God requires or forbids, we are free to act as we choose in the area in between.

When this question is put to Jesus, he sidesteps it. He does not challenge the fact that the scriptures (given through Moses) permitted divorce, but he goes back to an earlier part of the scriptures, revealing that God's intention is that there should be no divorce. How is this tension within the scriptures resolved? The point must be that the whole approach of 'define what God requires or forbids and we are free to do as we wish in the area in between' is wrong. God's desire is made clear in Genesis: God's desire is that marriage is permanent. Through Moses, however, laws were given to regulate the reality of a fallen world, including the need for divorce.

Where does that leave us? We still live in the fallen world for which Moses gave regulations. Presumably this means that there can be occasions when divorce is a sensible option, given the reality that all our hearts are 'hard' in different ways for all sorts of reasons. But divorce is always a falling short of God's desire for us; it will never simply be 'OK'.

It is also perhaps significant that Jesus goes back to the time before the fall. Many see this as highlighting the idea that in the kingdom brought by Jesus, we will return to a pre-fall state in which the regulations permitting divorce will no longer be needed. Some claim that now, within the church, our 'kingdom ethics' ought to match that pre-fall state, and divorce should not be allowed. But this seems to be ignoring the fact that the final transformation is still to come; until then, we still live in a world in which human hearts, our own included, are hard.

5 A house for the nations?

Mark 11:12–21

The placing of the action in the temple between the two halves of the incident with the fig tree is significant, for the fig tree represents Israel, or the temple system. Thus the plot of the fig tree is: (1) Jesus comes to Israel seeking fruit; (2) he doesn't find the fruit he is looking for; (3) he curses the tree and it withers. In this context we can then look at Jesus' arrival in Jerusalem. He goes to the temple, the heart of Israel. There he does not find what he is looking for, and so he 'curses' what he does find.

Sometimes this story is called the 'cleansing' of the temple, which can imply simply that the temple was being run in a corrupt fashion. However, the money changers and dove sellers were a necessary part of the temple's sacrificial system. Think of a prophet turning up at a church and throwing out all the hymn books and service sheets, saying, 'You have turned this place of worship into a library!' Similarly, when Jesus proclaims that it should be a 'house of prayer for all the nations' (v. 17), he is attacking the very fabric of the temple system, for this was the Jewish temple for the God who had chosen Israel alone out of the nations to be his special people. Thus Jesus' action is really a symbolic attack on the whole temple institution. (Note that 'robbers' in verse 17 is equally 'bandits' or 'terrorists', the word used to describe the nationalistic rebels against Rome, 40 years after Jesus. They had their headquarters at the temple, which was destroyed as a result.)

While taking this action, Jesus quotes the Old Testament (Isaiah 56:7), where it is said that in the future God will extend his favour to all who do his will, including 'foreigners' and other marginalised people. The action is also reminiscent of Malachi 3:1–2: 'The Lord whom you seek will suddenly come to his temple... But who can endure the day of his coming...? For he is like a refiner's fire.' Thus the incident with the fig tree makes clear the meaning of the temple incident. This was the final, symbolic moment when Jesus came to the religious system of his day, found it wanting because of its exclusivity, and proclaimed judgment against it.

At the same moment in Luke's Gospel (19:41–44), Jesus wept. This must be our own reaction to the way God's people managed to construct a system of worship and religious life that became exclusive and did not produce the fruit that God was looking for. Do we do any better?

6 The greatest commandment

Mark 12:28–34

We finish our brief look at Jesus and the law with this, Jesus' final piece of public teaching, which summarises his view of the law.

The first thing to notice is that here the Jewish scribe is praised and declared to be 'not far from the kingdom of God' (v. 34). Jesus may have said very stern things about aspects of religious life in his day, but there was also much that he approved—continuity as well as discontinuity.

The two commandments of love—love for God and love for neighbour —give a direction and pattern for the moral life, which appeals to many outside the Christian family. We should rejoice that there is this universal appeal in Jesus' words. However, this exchange hides a practical problem. A necessary feature of human society is that grand principles, like these love commands, need to be encapsulated in practical rules, customs and guidelines. The enquirer learning about the faith, when told to 'love God with all their heart, soul, mind and strength' is likely to ask, 'How?' and so we have practical rules, customs and guidelines such as 'burnt offerings and sacrifices' (v. 33) and other regulations (for example, on sabbath-keeping). How do grand principles and practical regulations re-late to each other?

The scribe says that the love commands are 'much more important' than the sacrifices (v. 33). Does this mean that the sacrifices are, nevertheless, still of some importance, or can they be discarded?

Presumably the answer is that all of these practical rules and customs should remain in place only while they actively contribute to the greater goal of loving God and neighbour, but this is to launch ourselves in a small boat on to a stormy sea. Life around us is always changing, so this approach would require us to be willing to keep on reassessing and changing the practical rules, customs and guidelines for moral living. Our only guiding star would be love for God and love for neighbour. This does seem to be what the early church did, reassessing fundamental rules and customs such as circumcision (laid down in the scriptures themselves as the essential mark of God's covenant: Genesis 17:10–14), in the light of the understanding that God relates to all people in the same way. Loving neighbour therefore meant removing the significance of the Jew–Gentile distinction (see, for example, Romans 3:27–31; 10:12–13). In the same way, which of our established rules, customs and guidelines for the Christian life is God calling us to reassess in the light of the commandments to love God and love neighbour?

Guidelines

We can avoid any challenge from this week's readings by saying that Jesus was only commenting on the Jewish law, and that since most of us don't follow it, his words don't concern us. The truth is, however, that much of his analysis would apply to the moral teaching, practice and customs of the church today as well, because he is, in truth, bringing a fundamental critique of any religious system of behaviour.

So, how flexible should rules be? Should we support those who follow them and shame those who don't, or support and welcome those who don't in the hope that, perhaps, at some unspecified time in the future, they might? Are religious rules, practices and customs important at all? Are they precious to us just because of history and the security they give us? Do they simply support a sense of exclusiveness? What would the world look like if everything was reassessed against the principles of love for God and neighbour? And do we believe that God forbids certain things, requires others, and that in the area in between we can do as we please (for example, 'I give to charity, I give to the church, I don't support immorality with my spending, so the rest is mine to do with as I want)? This is a catalogue of questions: ask God to show you one to ponder in more detail.

The death of Jesus

I The long shadow

Mark 3:1–6

Mark's Gospel has famously been called 'a passion narrative with a long introduction' (first by Martin Kähler in the 19th century). It is true that, from very early on, Jesus' approaching death overshadows the Gospel. In fact, today's passage is not even the first allusion to it, for in the parable of the bridegroom we read, 'The days will come when the bridegroom is taken away from them' (2:20): for anyone who knows how the story ends, this points us towards Jesus' death. Then, from the first passion prediction onwards (8:31), much of the second half of the Gospel is strongly coloured by the approaching trauma, until we arrive at 14:1: 'It was two days before the Passover…'

Today's passage comes at the end of a sequence of six 'conflict stories' in which Jesus has offended against established patterns of religion in his day. Indeed, a clash was highlighted right at the beginning, in the contrast between him and other teachers (1:22: 'he taught them as one having authority, and not as the scribes'). The statement that the leaders seek to destroy him (3:6) should be taken as a response to the whole sequence of passages, not just to this one. Nevertheless, why is this incident the 'final straw'?

Perhaps Jesus' offence had to do with his healing on the sabbath. Even on the pharisaic interpretation of the law, however, it is not clear that what Jesus did was 'work'. All he actually did was to speak (no touching or making ointment). There is a stronger case for arguing that the disciples' actions in the corn field (2:23) and Jesus' eating with sinners (2:15) broke the law, and words spoken earlier by Jesus threatened it more strongly (see 2:10 on forgiving sins and 2:27 on the significance of the sabbath). Perhaps the issue is that this incident was a very public confrontation, taking place on the sabbath in the synagogue. We could not find a more public and momentous arena for religious controversy: it's almost as if it was a set-up (v. 2). Jesus certainly responds by challenging his accusers openly and reacting with anger to their silence (vv. 4–5).

This confrontation is happening in Galilee, far from the temple, and in a land ruled by a Jewish king, Herod, not directly by the Romans. Thus the Pharisees and the Herodians (Herod's officers) represent religious and secular power combined. On the basis of this passage, they wish to kill Jesus not so much because of his teaching or even his actions, but because he is mounting a direct public challenge to their authority. This 'prophetic role' of challenging authority has been an important function of Jesus' disciples at various times in history. Is it now?

2 The death of John the Baptist

Mark 6:12–29

Jesus was closely connected with John the Baptist. Most historians would say that Jesus emerged from the movement surrounding John; certainly the Gospels give that impression (see, for example, Matthew 3:13–17; John 1:19–40). Here we learn that King Herod (the ruler of Galilee: we met his officers, the Herodians, in the previous passage) also believes that there is a connection—that, in fact, they are in some way the same person. We are then treated to the story of John's death. This is interesting (some might say that a bit of sex and violence always spices up a narrative) but why is it told here? What does it add to the story of Jesus?

John is a holy man who challenges important vested interests. They wish to stop him, but fear him because of his holiness. John also, we know, has an important public following. In the end, he is killed because those who hate him are able to manipulate the person in authority (Herod) in a shameful way. Herod doesn't really resist, and has John killed. This storyline is almost identical to that of Jesus, particularly during his last days in Jerusalem. He challenges the temple authorities and the religious establishment. They wish to stop him but fear the crowd. Therefore they manipulate Pilate in a shameful way—but Pilate also shows no interest in saving him and has him killed.

What difference do these parallels make? First, the story acts as a further 'passion prediction': as we read about John, we are reminded of what will happen to Jesus. Even though we are still in the first half of the Gospel, the shadow of the cross deepens. Second, it casts the events in Jerusalem into a certain light, suggesting that the actions of the Sanhedrin there should be seen not as 'trials' but as part of a manipulative process through which those whom Jesus has challenged (particularly the temple authorities) engineer his death. Pilate, through the lens of Herod, emerges as a pathetic figure, so tied up with his own reputation and the need to appear strong that it is possible for others to manipulate him. This is no whitewash of Pilate, for it would be a grave insult to any Roman governor to suggest that he was both as weak and as callous as is suggested of Herod here. It is a cleverly veiled way of commenting on Pilate.

Third, notice the one difference. John's disciples came and took his body away for burial: they stayed true to their master. Jesus' disciples fled and let a stranger bury him (Mark 15:43–46). Challenging power, manipulation and loyalty remain issues for us all today.

3 The passion predictions

Mark 10:32–34

Three times in Mark's Gospel, Jesus predicts his suffering, death and resurrection (see also 8:31; 9:31). The three occurrences are similar but not identical. Conventionally they are known as the 'passion predictions', although they talk not only of Jesus' passion (suffering) but also of his vindication and resurrection.

The word 'predictions' points to a difficulty posed by them in Gospels scholarship. Can we believe that Jesus predicted his death, or do we have to realise that the Gospels contain much that is post-Easter knowledge, put back into a pre-Easter setting? This idea might be uncontroversial if we are talking of material presented as interpretation or comment, such as the note 'Thus he declared all foods clean' in 7:19, but here we are talking about words directly attributed to Jesus.

We have to be careful. The Gospels were written after the first Easter, so it would be impossible for any Gospel writer not to be aware of 'how the story ends'. Furthermore, the material we have is clearly an edited version of what happened. Jesus would have been a very peculiar figure if, on the road, he actually said only these 61 words (although of course he would have spoken Aramaic, and the best we have is a Gospel written in Greek). That process of remembering, editing and translating happened after the resurrection, so it would be unsurprising to see some post-Easter influence.

It is not impossible, though, for someone to predict that they are likely to die. Given all that had happened in Galilee, if Jesus was approaching Jerusalem with the intention of attacking the temple at Passover in the way that he did, without trying to hide himself, a sentence of death would be a fair prediction. We need also to examine the 'Son of Man' title, which appears to be Jesus' self-description of choice and which, in various places, is linked explicitly to Daniel 7 (see Mark 13:26; 14:62–63). Daniel 7 is a story of the people of God, represented by a human figure ('son of man'), undergoing great suffering before they are vindicated by God. If this text guided Jesus' sense of his mission, then a prediction of suffering followed by vindication is hardly surprising.

Aside from such historical questions, how does this passage affect us? For me, the challenge is in the contrast between Jesus' courage and the fearfulness of those (like me) who follow him (v. 32). We know that in the end God will vindicate us, just as he did Jesus, yet would we have the courage to face suffering? I hardly seem to have the courage to face a bit of discomfort.

4 Jesus' death: a ransom

Mark 10:42—45

The famous statement of the purpose behind Jesus' death—'to give his life as a ransom for many'—occurs at the end of Jesus' discussion of status, power and servanthood, occasioned by James' and John's request to sit at Jesus' right and left in his glory. The rest of this passage was discussed as part of our consideration of discipleship in the last edition; here we will focus on this final saying about 'ransom'.

Books have been written on this one verse. We will focus on four possible meanings of the phrase. First, there is a connection point in the literature circulating in Jesus' day about the Maccabean martyrs (who died 200 years earlier). 2 Maccabees 7:37–38 says, 'I, like my brothers, give up body and life for the laws of our ancestors... to bring to an end the wrath of the Almighty that has justly fallen on our whole nation.' The idea that death might achieve the purpose of a person's life was not alien within the Judaism of Jesus' day. Against this background, Jesus' death is solving the problem of God's anger at the nation's sin. Second, the word 'to ransom/redeem' is used in the Old Testament to describe God's rescue of the people from Egypt. This links what Jesus is doing to the great act of salvation in the Old Testament that led to the formation of the Jewish people. Third, another possible background to 'ransom' is the slave market. This brings in the idea of a payment made to 'buy out' another person from slavery (as opposed to the exodus, which uses the word 'redeem' in a rather more vague sense, effectively equivalent to 'save'). Finally, some see a connection with the 'suffering servant' of Isaiah, particularly Isaiah 53 (see, for example, verse 12: 'he bore the sin of many'.

What can we make of these multiple possible connections? Some commentators argue at great length to decide which of them is 'correct'—although it is not clear what 'correct' means. If, when Jesus said these words (or when Mark wrote them), they were not intended as a link to the exodus, does that mean God cannot speak to us now through that link, particularly because it is suggested later by Jesus' death at the Passover? It is more fruitful to allow these meanings to sit alongside each other as we contemplate the multifaceted nature of Jesus' death, united in the idea that it was a willing death, borne for others, and achieving a great rescue.

5 Jesus' death: a new covenant

Mark 14:22–25

Eucharistic theology is one of the richest interfaces between spirituality and theology. Here, however, we will focus on the bare words given to us in Mark's Gospel. They are very limited. It is a Passover meal (14:16–17), an important night in which God's rescue of his people from slavery in Egypt is remembered. It would be an exaggeration to say that it was re-enacted, but nevertheless the Passover meal included many symbolic actions and rituals. It is in this context that we should understand what Jesus does and says.

What happens with the bread is very limited: it is a single loaf, broken and shared, with the words 'This is my body.' What would this mean? It becomes clearer when we get to the cup, for here we are given more detail: it is not just his blood but is also 'of the covenant' and is 'poured out for many' (v. 24). Jesus is enacting a new covenant ritual. The phrase 'blood of the covenant' occurs in Exodus 24:8, when the covenant between God and those he rescued in the Passover is sealed in blood at Sinai (see also Zechariah 9:11). But here there are two distinctive features. First, the blood is said to be Jesus', and in this context we can see the sharing of the body as also signifying his death. Jesus is enacting a new covenant ritual in which he is the sacrifice. Second, it is 'for many'. It is hard to pin this phrase down, but it conveys expansiveness: this covenant is for more than just the disciples, for more than just a small group or even, perhaps, than just the Jewish people (compare 10:45).

35

This is a covenant marked by its breadth, not its limitation. Furthermore, logically this must be a 'new covenant' that points us to Old Testament prophecy such as Jeremiah 31:31–34. This prophecy claims that the new covenant will be better than the one at the exodus, for it will bring forgiveness of sins and a new intimacy between people and God.

The final oath (v. 25) intensifies the whole, for it brings a sense of imminence. Something—the arrival of the kingdom of God—must happen soon, for wine drinking was a regular part of life. Jesus and his disciples have arrived in Jerusalem, and it is Passover. Now is the moment! The kingdom of God is a complex theme. It starts 'near' in 1:15 and some will see it before they taste death (9:1), and in some sense Mark claims that it 'came' in the events of Jesus' death and resurrection.

6 Jesus' death: darkness

Mark 15:15–37

Finally we reach the actual account of Jesus' death. (Note: we have stopped short of verses 38–39 because we examined their revelation of Jesus' identity in the last edition.) Within the richness and horror of this passage, I would draw attention to three points. First, we ought to take in the repulsive, horrendous suffering: the casual mention of flogging (v. 15), sufficient on its own to kill, the piercing with thorns (v. 17), the mockery (vv. 18–19, 29–32), and finally the long, slow, agonising suffocation of crucifixion itself (v. 24).

Second, we notice the theological irony in the passage. Jesus is proclaimed 'King of the Jews' by both the Romans and the temple authorities (vv. 18, 26, 32). They think that the title is laughably ironic, since how could a dying man be king? Perhaps we think the same—that Jesus can only be king when the shame of the cross is wiped away by resurrection. Or is this cross truly his throne? Similarly, the ideas that he would destroy the temple, be the Messiah and save others are thrown back at him. These ideas were in the air and provided the context for his arrest, trial and condemnation, but again it is assumed that his execution proves those claims false. It is a picture of the finality of death—death making a mockery of all our hopes and dreams.

Third, there is the darkness—physical darkness (v. 33) but, more importantly, spiritual darkness (v. 34) as Jesus cries out that he has been forsaken. Some commentators attempt to 'rewrite' this spiritual anguish, claiming that since this is the first line from Psalm 22, Jesus really had in mind the hopeful way in which the psalm ends. But if that was the meaning we were to take, why not quote the end? No, if we read the text straightforwardly, we see Jesus experiencing the horror of feeling utterly alone and forsaken, even by the God he called 'father', whose will he accepted (14:36). Gone is the confidence of the passion predictions, as the true horror of a pain-filled, torturous death is faced.

How can we respond? First with thankfulness and awe at the depth of love that was willing to endure even this to restore our relationship with God. But we are also reminded of the character-destroying pain that is caused by insults and apparent failure. We see it often enough in our media; maybe we know people going through similar experiences; maybe we have suffered it ourselves. There is no answer but one consolation—that in such experiences we model Christ.

Guidelines

Jesus' death is so enormous—so central to Christianity, its theology, spirituality and mission—that it is hard to give a simple point for further thought. Three areas have emerged this week:

• The need for us to follow Jesus' example in challenging power, despite what it might cost us.
• The nature of Jesus' sacrifice and the expansive rescue it achieved.
• The pain that insult and failure bring, and yet the reality of God's presence with us throughout.

Perhaps one of these areas would repay further thought and meditation.

FURTHER READING

James R. Edwards, *The Gospel According to Mark*, Apollos, 2002.
Dick France, *Mark* (The People's Bible Commentary), BRF, 1998.
Morna D. Hooker, *The Gospel According to St Mark*, Continuum, 2001.
Donald Michie, David Rhoads and Joanna Dewey, *Mark as a Story: An Introduction to the Narrative of a Gospel*, Augsburg Fortress, 1999.
Tom Wright, *Mark for Everyone*, SPCK, 2001.

2 SAMUEL

Despite its title, Samuel is neither the author nor the subject of this book: it is concerned entirely with King David. Samuel's story ended in 1 Samuel 25, and David's story began in 1 Samuel 16, even while Saul, Israel's first king, was still on the throne. 2 Samuel starts with the aftermath of Saul's death and David's accession to the throne.

The two books of Samuel relate to an important period in Israel's history: the transition from a loose federation of disparate tribes to a society united under a king and strong enough to withstand the powerful Philistine threat. The main part of 2 Samuel falls into two distinct sections, first David's rise to power (chs. 1—8), then the vexed question of his successor (chs. 9—20), which concludes in 1 Kings 1—2. These latter chapters are often known as the Succession Narrative since they describe the struggle for the throne within David's family. Here David himself appears a troubled figure, torn helplessly between his commitments as king and parent. There is little overt reference to God's intervention in this story of human scheming for power.

It is a complex story of loyalty and deceit, of divine calling and lust for power, of humility and arrogant manipulation for selfish ends, of a ruthless monarch and an emotional father. There are high points, such as David's lament for Saul and Jonathan, and low points of sheer brutality and senseless destruction of life. Then the tone changes abruptly as we near the end of the book, with a long and beautiful psalm of praise (ch. 22; Psalm 18 in the Psalter). The book concludes with an appendix (chs. 23—24).

These notes are based on the New Revised Standard Version.

1 'How the mighty have fallen!'

2 Samuel 1

The final chapter of 1 Samuel ended on a sombre note with Israel's defeat at the hands of the Philistines and the humiliating treatment of its dead king, Saul—a pitiful story redeemed only by the devotion of the men of Jabesh-gilead in giving him honourable burial. Significantly, 2 Samuel begins straight away with a contradictory account of Saul's death.

Here is the first instance of deception in this story, which is fraught with subterfuge. A messenger (an Amalekite from a bedouin people in the south of Canaan, now resident in Israel), motivated by self-interest and eager to gain credit with the new king, brings David the symbols of royalty taken from Saul's corpse. David, distraught at the tragic news of the death of Saul his erstwhile enemy and of Jonathan his close friend, to whom in the past he owed his life (1 Samuel 19:1–7), checks the authenticity of the report. Retribution is swift.

There are two points of particular interest in this opening chapter: first, David's famous lament over Saul and Jonathan, and second, the sanctity of the king's person as the Lord's anointed (vv. 14, 16). Two incidents earlier in the story illustrate this latter point. David, even as a hunted fugitive fleeing from Saul's anger, refused to lift his hand against the Lord's anointed, guilt-stricken even at having cut a corner from the king's robe (1 Samuel 24:4–6, 10; 26:8–9). Such was the king's status in ancient Israel—although, as we shall see, he was equally subject to God's law as were his people.

David's is a complex character. Courageous in battle, he is at heart a peacemaker. The exquisite beauty of his lament in verses 19–27, its emotional outpouring and generous praise of Saul his enemy (v. 24), have rightly made it famous. Ashkelon and Gath (v. 20) were two of the five Philistine cities along the Mediterranean coast, another being Gaza, a name familiar today and sadly still a place of conflict.

2 The first step in David's kingship

2 Samuel 2:1–17, 24–28

The rivalry between the northern tribes and Judah, later to result in permanent schism, is even now apparent. David's own tribe, Judah, anoints him king in Hebron but already he has wider ambitions, hence his less than subtle approach to the men of Jabesh-gilead, the very people who, at personal risk, had given Saul honourable burial (1 Samuel 31:11–13). There is, too, an obvious successor to Saul—his son Ishbaal.

For several years David has to be content with a limited kingdom, until he becomes king over the whole nation in 2 Samuel 5.

The personal rivalry between Ishbaal and David provokes a contest in what at first looks like a sporting event (the Hebrew translated 'contest' in verse 14 suggests 'to sport, play'). Not so the gruesome end! Life was held cheap. Yet this is not a simple story of good and bad, a story slanted in favour of David's supporters. It is life in the raw, a realistic portrayal of complex human nature. Abner, David's opponent, initiated the bloody contest, and he it is whose common sense ends the ensuing slaughter (v. 26). Notice the reference here to the kinship of north and south, a significant factor even after the rupture into two separate kingdoms, following the death of Solomon. But the seeds of bitterness had been sown. There was a long war between the rival houses of Saul and David, though the latter was already in the ascendant (3:1).

Time and again the biblical story illustrates the futility of battle. Violence begets violence, and today's world is no different. Yet out of this maelstrom of human folly and ambition, God continued to work out his purposes. And so it is that, in the midst of our equally violent and tumultuous world, we continue to pray in faith, 'Thy kingdom come, thy will be done.'

3 Political intrigue and shifting loyalties

2 Samuel 3:12–39

David does not come out well from this story. He is manipulative and despotic, intent only on his own advantage. Abner is untrustworthy, siding with David simply in anger against Ishbaal, his former protégé. Nor is he averse to turning the 'word of the Lord' to his own ends (v. 18). God's promise to David had been conveniently overlooked by Abner in his bid for Saul's son to rule over the northern tribes. Now it serves his purpose better to remember it. David is easily persuaded and grasps at Abner's offer. As Abner knows only too well, this is what his heart desires.

So David negotiates with Abner. Michal, Saul's daughter, formerly David's wife (1 Samuel 18:25–29, itself a disreputable story), is for him nothing but a bargaining counter. Yet not everyone at that time regarded women as mere chattels to be treated without respect or compassion. David's shameful attitude to Michal is set in unrelieved contrast to her husband's genuine devotion and love. The touching human story is submerged in the overriding political intrigue. David's motive is not hard to discern. In this way he prevents any future child of Michal from becoming a rival for the kingdom.

The 'heroes' of the Old Testament story are not whitewashed. They are complex flesh-and-blood characters, capable of selfish political intrigue and, at times, of surprising loyalty.

Human affairs were no simpler then than now. Joab, David's faithful general, is aghast at his sudden reliance on Abner, against whom Joab has a personal grudge for the murder of his brother Asahel (2:23). Joab's treacherous action in killing Abner is understandable. What is more surprising is David's reaction, first in uttering a violent curse on Joab's family (v. 29), and most of all in his lament at Abner's graveside. Was this a sign of sincere respect for a brave man or, more insidiously, anxiety lest, with Abner gone, northern Israel's ties with Judah would be weakened and David's kingship threatened? David keeps his own hands clean of Abner's death with a strangely feeble admission that events are out of control: 'Today I am powerless, even though anointed king; these men, the sons of Zeruiah, are too violent for me' (v. 39).

Where is God in all this? It is a thought-provoking exercise to compare David's desire for divine vengeance (v. 39b) with Psalm 51, the famous penitential psalm attributed to David.

4 David becomes king over all Israel

2 Samuel 5:1–12

It was a historic moment when David was anointed king in Hebron over his own southern tribe, Judah. Now, by general agreement, his realm extends to take in the ten northern tribes together with Benjamin (Saul's tribe), which lay on the borders of Judah. Thus, for a time, north and south were held together under a united monarchy. But the relationship was only skin-deep. It fell apart finally after Solomon's death and, for two centuries, Judah and Israel continued as separate kingdoms, sometimes friendly, sometimes hostile. Eventually, towards the end of the eighth century, Assyria overran the northern kingdom. But right from the start the union was fragile, as we shall see.

For the moment, the northern tribes claim kinship with David and, with a touch of flattery, acknowledge his prowess under divine direction. This is a willing acceptance of David's rule, ratified by covenant, but repudiated later more than once when it suited them (for example, see 20:1). The king is described as 'shepherd' (v. 2), caring for the welfare of his people, for the king was ideally the earthly agent of God's rule, dispensing his justice for the poor and oppressed (Psalm 74:1–4).

Hebron was now too closely identified, by its geographical position, with the tribe of Judah. The need was pressing to establish a capital equally acceptable to both north and south. Thus Jerusalem, originally a Jebusite stronghold, strategically situated and independent of both northern and southern tribes, enters history. The Jebusites were scathing, secure in their fortress (v. 6), but their boasts proved empty. The method by which it was captured for David is not entirely clear. The Hebrew word translated in verse 8 as 'water shaft' occurs elsewhere only in Psalm 42:7, where 'cataracts' (NRSV, REB) is a more appropriate meaning, referring to the 'sluices' of heaven.

David prospers. For the moment, there is peace in the surrounding area. A friendly ruler, Hiram king of Tyre, supplies materials for his palace. But soon the Philistine forces threaten again—though eventually David emerges victorious.

5 The ark installed in Jerusalem

2 Samuel 6

To set this incident in context, we must look back to 1 Samuel 7:1–2. The ark has been lodged for the last 20 years at the house of Abinadab in Kiriath-jearim, about seven miles north-west of Jerusalem. Much of 1 Samuel 4—6 is devoted to a collection of highly theological stories about the ark's significance as a symbol of God's presence and awesome power. These stories gave warning, too, that it was no automatic guarantee of his presence with Israel. The Lord is sovereign and free and what matters supremely is his people's commitment and obedience. No material object or external ritual can ever guarantee his presence among his people.

Here in today's reading, the ark is described, in somewhat allusive language, as 'called by the name of the Lord of hosts who is enthroned on the cherubim' (v. 2), a reminder both of the power of the divine name and of his glorious otherness. Philistine control had been weakened and now David was able to bring the ark to Jerusalem, astutely making this city not only the political but also the religious centre of his kingdom.

All does not go according to plan. The strange death of Uzzah (whatever rational explanation is offered) is, above all, a reminder that holy things are not to be treated lightly. David is terrified and offloads responsibility for this dangerous object to someone else. Once again, David, motivated by self-interest, doesn't come well out of this incident. Later, encouraged by the evident blessing brought to Obed-edom's household, David transfers the ark triumphantly and joyfully into Jerusalem.

The happy occasion ends with festivities for all the people, but someone is less than happy. Michal, David's wife, despises his unrestrained dancing 'before the Lord' (v. 14). She sees not worship but vulgarity, a lowering of the royal dignity. But is there also a deeper motive behind her reaction, a hidden agenda of bitterness against the 'usurper' of her father's throne, as David's angry response suggests? Where is the 'soft answer' that 'turns away wrath' (Proverbs 15:1)? This is a thoroughly human story of fraught emotions. The reason for Michal's future childlessness is left ambiguous. Was it understood by the writer as divine displeasure or simply the outcome of David's anger?

6 Seeds of the messianic hope

2 Samuel 7:1–21

There are two main points of interest in this chapter: its attitude to the building of a temple for God, who in earlier times had shared his people's wilderness journeys, and the close relationship of Israel's king to God, expressed as son to father by virtue of his office (v. 14), which was to develop eventually into the expectation of a Messiah.

Verses 1–7 are interesting in the light of divergent attitudes to the temple expressed in several parts of the Old Testament. Sometimes the temple is regarded as the all-important central sanctuary, unifying the worship of Yahweh and consecrated by his presence (Psalm 84). Elsewhere strong opposition is voiced against the building of an earthly sanctuary for the Lord of all the earth, since 'heaven is my throne and the earth is my footstool' (Isaiah 66:1–3). Interestingly, Solomon's prayer at the eventual consecration of the temple amalgamates both ideas: 'Will God indeed dwell on the earth? Even heaven and the highest heaven cannot contain you, much less this house that I have built' (1 Kings 8:27).

In today's reading there is certainly hesitation about establishing a fixed locality as God's 'dwelling' (vv. 5–7). The contrast between Nathan's immediate human reaction (v. 3) and the ensuing 'word of the Lord' (v. 4) is notable. (We might perhaps compare the distinction made in Paul's epistles between his own advice and the compelling word from the Lord: 1 Corinthians 7:10 contrasted with verse 12.) God is a journeying God, present wherever his people are, a truth emphasised by Ezekiel when the dispirited people were deported to Babylon. Although far from homeland and temple, they were not cut off from the Lord—an encouragement in our own experiences of dislocation.

Verses 14–16 are significant for Israel's ideology of kingship, which was seen as a position of both privilege and responsibility. The Davidic line continued until 587BC, disrupted eventually by the exile to Babylon, but this promise became the basis of the messianic hope so eagerly awaited in New Testament times and fulfilled in Christ (Hebrews 1:1–5). David's response to God's promises was praise and worship—and humility.

Reflect on David's words, 'courage to pray this prayer' (v. 27)—a salutary reminder for us today, as we rejoice in God's promises, to come in prayer not presumptuously but in humble gratitude.

Guidelines

A fascinating story has been woven of the rise and fall of leaders, a story sometimes of courage and often of self-serving ambition in life's vicissitudes. We have seen David's rule extended beyond his own tribe of Judah, and a new capital established at Jerusalem, with lasting repercussions down to the present day. Out of flawed human nature came a reaching after God, the desire to establish worship at the centre of the nation's life. But in the end our vision was lifted beyond the immediate to the messianic hope fulfilled in Jesus. Above the welter of political struggle and personal ambition rose David's great prayer of praise and thanksgiving. We cannot do better than echo his words of praise: 'O Lord God, you are God, and your words are true' (v. 28). In these words is our hope for today's troubled world.

1 Generosity or political scheming?

2 Samuel 9

Chapter 9 brings us to what is generally regarded as a distinct section within 2 Samuel. Often known as the Succession Narrative or Court History, it extends through chapters 9—20 and into 1 Kings 1—2. It is the story of serious conflict and intrigue within the royal house as one after another of David's sons strives for the throne. For David personally, there is conflict between his responsibilities as king and his emotions as parent. Outwardly, however, after the previous battles all seems well. David's rule is just and fair (8:15).

Whether the record is contemporary with the events described is debatable, and scholars are divided on this point. Its theological standpoint seems somewhat distinctive, presenting not so much an interventionist God, as elsewhere in Samuel, but 'divine immanence and horizontal causality' (R.P. Gordon, *1 and 2 Samuel*), although it must be noted that at decisive turning points God does intervene directly (11:27; 12:24; 17:14).

By the end of chapter 8, David has established his rule over all Israel, both north and south. Now we have an account of David's generosity to Saul's grandson Mephibosheth, showing him kindness for Jonathan his father's sake. Mephibosheth, away in Lo-debar east of the Jordan, is to be welcomed into the king's household. He responds with servility in colourful oriental court language (v. 8), an echo of David's self-deprecation before Saul ('A dead dog? A single flea?' 1 Samuel 24:14).

Was David motivated simply by generosity and his erstwhile love for

Jonathan, or by paranoia, fearing that Mephibosheth would head a rival faction among Saul's descendants? The narrator's double emphasis on Mephibosheth's disability (vv. 3, 14; see 4:4) seems to preclude him as a rallying point of opposition, but David's action was politically shrewd as well as generous. Was Mephibosheth's welcome into the royal household, together with his young son, a kind of genteel house arrest? There may be more to this apparently simple kindness than meets the eye on first reading. Ziba (servant of Saul) and his family are to administer Mephibosheth's estates, ostensibly on his behalf. However, since David will provide for him, presumably Ziba's own family will be the beneficiaries, thus securing their loyalty to David. As often, human nature is complex and motives rarely simple.

2 David and Bathsheba

2 Samuel 11

The scene is set for this disturbing story. It is spring, the advantageous time for doing battle. Joab, at the head of David's army, is gaining ground, laying siege to Rabbah, modern Amman, capital of Jordan. Suddenly the sequence of tenses is broken, starkly in Hebrew: 'But David stayed/sat in Jerusalem'—an inactive king, resting and strolling in the cool evening, enjoying luxury and ease in contrast with life on the battlefield. Not for nothing do verses 1 and 2 stand in dramatic contrast.

This is a tragic story about the misuse of power. Nothing stands in David's way. From his house on the hill he sees below him the huddled houses and crowded courtyards of the people—and Bathsheba. Sexual immorality is compounded with murder, sin upon sin. The interplay of diverse motives is intriguing. David's motives in summoning Uriah from the battlefield and bidding him go home to his wife are clear enough. Uriah's are less so in his refusal to accommodate the king. Does he speak as a loyal soldier committed to share the hardships of battle, or are his words in verse 11 a veiled criticism of the king's life of ease? Even more uncertain, is he aware of the king's adultery with his wife? Hints are there for the reader to ponder. And here is the essence of tragedy. Uriah, through his loyalty and high ideals, effects his own destruction.

There is now no escape for David. He cannot conceal his guilt by passing off the unborn child as Uriah's. The language of verse 27, blunt enough in the English translation, '[he] brought her to his house', is starker still in Hebrew: 'he gathered her into his house' as if merely one possession among many.

Was Bathsheba complicit in the adultery? The question is left unresolved. She had probably little say in what the king demanded but the matter remains ambiguous in the interchange of two words for 'husband' in verse 26. When she heard that her husband (*'ish*) was dead, she 'mourned her *ba'al* (master, lord)'. Are the words synonymous or is there deliberate irony here? Amid this web of adultery and murder, of ease, luxury and uncontrolled lust on David's part, God is not absent. The narrative ends not with the child's birth but with the Lord's verdict: literally, 'What David had done was evil in the Lord's eyes.'

3 Nathan's parable strikes home

2 Samuel 12:1–14

The last chapter ended with David 'sending' for Bathsheba, now free, as a widow, to become his wife legitimately. But there is another actor in the drama. Now it is the Lord who 'sends' through his prophet. Nathan confronts the king. His tale is dramatic and heart-rending—and, for David, immensely disturbing.

Notice the high standing of prophet in relation to the monarch at this period, a status that commanded respect. With time, this diminished: hence King Jehoiakim's arrogant treatment of both Jeremiah and his message several centuries later (Jeremiah 36:22–26). Noteworthy, too, is the prophet's presentation of his message as a parable. The king, at times so ruthless, finds his emotions stirred by the poignant tale and angrily demands justice for the wrong done by the rich to the poor. The hammer blow falls: 'You are the man!' (v. 7). David, shepherd of his people (5:2), has pronounced uncompromising judgment on himself. He, no less than his people, is subject to God's law and is held accountable.

Nathan's mode of delivering the Lord's word, implicating the guilty in his own condemnation, is not unique. Isaiah's famous ballad of the vineyard (5:1–7) likewise calls on his audience to pronounce judgment against the unfruitful vineyard. Not until verses 6c–7 does it become apparent that the vineyard's owner is the Lord and they themselves are the worthless vineyard.

Every action brings its consequences. There is forgiveness for the penitent David (v. 13), but forgiveness does not cancel out the effects of sin. Despite David's persistent and agonised pleading for his son's life, the child dies. The bald statement in verse 14 shocks us. Yet isn't it still a fact of life that often the innocent, even the unborn child, suffers the consequences of another's guilt or self-gratification, caught up in the tangle of life? The event doesn't leave David unscathed. His sorrow is palpable. His immorality and ruthless cruelty were more than a crime against Bathsheba and Uriah. 'You have utterly scorned the Lord,' says the prophet (v. 14).

4 David's fatherly love

2 Samuel 12:15–25

The Old Testament writer sees the Lord's hand in this bereavement. For him, whatever befell, whether for blessing or disaster, nothing was outside the Lord's control. In this lay the seeds of hope, the ground of confidence. For Israel, even in the trauma of exile in Babylon, all was in God's hands. The God who could bring judgment on his wayward people could also bring them salvation.

David doesn't take the sad outcome of his sin lightly. Distressed and penitent, he fasts and pleads for the child's life, displaying the same depths of anguish as he was to do later at the death of his adult son Absalom (18:33). He shows himself an emotional, compassionate father—yet there had been no glimmer of compassion for the brave and loyal soldier Uriah, whom he had so cruelly wronged. Then he was simply the despotic king intent on his own selfish pleasure. Such is the complexity of human personality.

While there is still hope, David prays—seven days of grief until the child dies. But David doesn't wallow in his sorrow. He makes a new start, beginning with worship. Is there, perhaps, in this passage a glimpse of belief in the afterlife, so rare in the Old Testament—the hope of reunion after death? David shares Bathsheba's sorrow. There is a future, a new child, Solomon. Once again Nathan comes as the Lord's messenger, this time with a word of blessing and a new name for the child, Jedidiah, 'Beloved of the Lord'. It comes, then, as no surprise when, despite much scheming by David's other sons, Solomon eventually succeeds to the throne.

It was noted in the introduction that there is little overt reference to the Lord's intervention in human affairs in chapters 9—20, the Succession Narrative. This is not the case in our readings yesterday and today. It is significant that, amid this disaster of sin and death, Nathan is twice sent by the Lord, first to the sinner in rebuke, then to the sorrowing with hope for the future in the assurance of the Lord's love.

5 A devious enterprise

2 Samuel 14:1–30

Once again, a woman—nameless, like other women earlier in the story—appears on the scene and makes a dramatic impact on the course of events. Joab stops at nothing to achieve his aim of bringing his favourite, Absalom, back from exile to the seat of power in Jerusalem. His loyalty to Absalom is unwavering, his deceit unlimited.

The woman is courageous. Her identification as 'a wise woman' (v. 2) implies some kind of public recognition within her own community, possibly that she was gifted with fluent speech and the ability to tell a moving story, as Nathan was. She approaches the king with her tragic tale of two sons, one dead at his brother's hands, the other liable to the death penalty for homicide, and she a widow. Regardless of strict justice, the king, in extravagant language, grants a reprieve to the guilty son (v. 11). The parallel to David's two sons in the previous chapter, where Absalom murdered his elder brother Amnon, is obvious to the reader.

We have here an interesting insight into the king's role in securing justice and protection for a harassed individual, and into a citizen's right of direct access to the king to present a petition. Like Nathan before her, the woman doesn't soften the blow: 'the king convicts himself' (v. 13). David understands immediately. Joab's scheming is behind it. The woman is sycophantic. Piling flattery on flattery (vv. 17, 19, 20), she discloses the whole business. The upshot is Absalom's return from exile, though still debarred from the king's presence for two more years (v. 28).

But the story is not yet finished. The fulsome description of Absalom's outstanding beauty inserted here (vv. 25–26) hints at more drama to come.

Meanwhile, Joab is dilatory in supporting Absalom's plans. In return, Absalom provokes Joab to action by committing arson against his property, despite Joab's previous support. Sadly, as often when the stakes are high, gratitude is short-lived and self-interest predominates.

6 Loyalty versus disloyalty

2 Samuel 15:1–14, 19–23

The last chapter ended in heightened drama, the long-delayed reconciliation of son to father: 'the king kissed Absalom' (14:33). Other kisses were soon to follow, kisses of disloyalty (15:5). There are several significant points to note in this story of Absalom's rebellion. First, a hint that David had been negligent in one of his primary roles, that of administering justice for the needy and oppressed (see Psalm 72). Had there been no grounds for Absalom's accusation (v. 3), his seditious plan would scarcely have succeeded. It was a plot nurtured patiently for four long years, and thus he 'stole the hearts of the people' (v. 6). Winning hearts and minds was as crucial then as now.

Why did Absalom choose Hebron as the place for proclaiming his rival kingship? It was his birthplace and the original centre of support for David against Saul's heir, Ishbaal. Absalom laid his plans carefully. Many of those invited to go with him 'went in their innocence' (v. 11). But there is a bigger problem in this story: why did David flee so precipitately without offering resistance? Had he lost heart? There is a surprising, not insignificant detail in David's conversation with Ittai towards the end of our passage. Testing Ittai's determination to accompany him, David describes Absalom as 'the king' (v. 19), although twice Ittai affirms David's right to the title (v. 21). This is an unusual portrayal of David, hitherto a man of courage and determination. Now weakened (by the tension between his roles as king and father?) and lacking the heart to resist, he vacates Jerusalem, lamented by his loyal people.

Ironically, history repeats itself in reverse. David came from wilderness to throne; now he is back in the wilderness. But, as the story continues, we see that history has moved on. The days when the ark journeyed with God's wilderness people are long gone. The ark belongs in Jerusalem at the heart of the nation (v. 25). David, still wily, sends with it his loyal supporters, the priests Zadok and Abiathar. Once again the chapter ends on a dramatic note. Absalom, newly proclaimed king, enters his capital city, Jerusalem. But so does Hushai, David's friend and spy (v. 35). For the ancient writer, Absalom's revolt was of prime importance, to judge by the space given to it (chs. 15—20). Absalom was not 'the Lord's anointed'. The throne was not at human disposal. The succession had yet to be resolved.

Guidelines

As we began this week's readings, David's kingdom had been established over the tribes of both north and south. Since then we have watched a struggle of a different kind within the royal house itself. We have seen David's weakness as father override his judgment as king, his un-controlled passion for Bathsheba result in his deliberate crime against the brave and loyal Uriah, and through it all the tragic consequences of wrong choices. No one, not even the king himself, is exempt from accountability towards God. Writ large over this complex narrative is the importance of wise and honourable choice—decisions made not from personal ambition or blind emotion but for the good of all.

Here the story is of universal relevance despite the passing of centuries. Whatever our situation in life or our responsibilities, we cannot evade the constant need to make wise and generous choices. Only by God's grace and the controlling power of the Holy Spirit are we delivered from the devastating consequences of selfish, misguided decisions.

'Lead me, O Lord, in your righteousness... make your way straight before me' (Psalm 5:8).

1 David in exile

2 Samuel 16:1–14

Loyalties are divided, some for and some against the king in his voluntary exile, others perhaps with self-interest paramount. The story rings true to life: Ziba with self-serving loyalty, Shimei with undisguised hostility, and Abishai ever hot-tempered and eager for vengeance (see 3:30, 39). Most interesting of all is the glimpse we have into David's theology (vv. 10–12). Ziba knows where his advantage lies, switches sides and unashamedly curries favour with David. Previously a supporter of Mephibosheth, Saul's grandson and heir, he now casts suspicion on Mephibosheth's motives (v. 3). But another claimant to the throne has already entered the contest—Absalom, David's disloyal son.

David makes a facile promise to give Ziba all that Mephibosheth had inherited from Saul, but it is an empty promise. We know already that Ziba had been given control of Saul's lands, ostensibly for Mephibosheth's benefit (9:9–10) but in reality for Ziba himself, since Mephibosheth was to be David's permanent guest. Thus Ziba's apparent generosity to David (vv. 1–2) seems, on second thoughts, to be disingenuous and self-serving, as also is David's promise to Ziba.

Shimei, another of Saul's supporters, is more honest and more dangerous in his open hostility, rejoicing in David's misfortunes as due retribution for usurping (as he sees it) Saul's throne. David's reaction is surprising. He refuses to meet violence with violence, confident in the Lord's ultimate control of events. The king appears a broken man, trudging on foot with his men away from Jerusalem while Shimei keeps pace with them on a hillside, hurling stones and dust with curses at the anointed king. David's confidence is in the Lord for ultimate good, though whether this will be a reversal of his present 'distress' (v. 12, NRSV) or forgiveness of his 'iniquity' (NRSV footnote) is not entirely clear.

There is more to come of Shimei's story later. Spared by David on oath but only during his own lifetime, Shimei finally meets a violent end in 1 Kings 2:36–46.

2 Absalom's tragic death

2 Samuel 18:1–18

This is a fascinating story of contrasts. First, there is the conflict of emotions in David as king exercising military authority and as father yearning for his favourite son; second, we see a contrast between the loyalty of a common soldier and the defiant disloyalty of the ruthless general, Joab. In both respects it is a very human story.

David's dilemma clouds his judgment. Involved at the same time as both king and father, he sends his troops into battle tragically against his own son Absalom. The heroes of the Old Testament are not 'plaster saints' but flawed heroes caught in the tangle of life. Such is David, the king.

David's troops are deployed against Absalom's men across the Jordan, at that time a thickly forested area. The slaughter was massive. In brief but telling words, 'the forest claimed more victims that day than the sword' (v. 8). David, courageous as ever, is deterred from entering the fray by wise advice. As the army marches to battle, his heart speaks (v. 5). Affection for his son goes deep: 'deal gently for my sake with the young man Absalom.' Events take a tragi-comic turn. Absalom's great pride, his magnificent hair (14:25–26), is his downfall. For him, nemesis swiftly follows hubris.

There was no mistaking David's orders, heard by troops and officers alike—a necessary prelude to what follows. The unidentified soldier shows unquestioning loyalty. No hope of personal gain tempts him to flout his king's authority (v. 12). The interplay between this unnamed man and Joab is worth reflecting on. Joab, a prominent figure in the narrative, an honoured general commanding David's forces, has no such scruples. Here is no loyalty to the king, only sheer brutality. In cold blood he strikes the helpless, still living victim through the heart (revenge, perhaps, for Absalom's high-handed treatment of Joab's property in 14: 30). Absalom's humiliation is complete in the manner both of his death and of his burial.

So ends the story of the king's rebellious son, but, for David, the emotional tension between his commitments as king and as bereaved father is not yet over.

3 Emotion clouds David's judgment

The gut-wrenching turmoil caused by the conflict between a king's responsibility and a father's affection well-nigh destroys David. Eager for news from the battlefield, his thought is only for Absalom's safety. The many who have risked their lives in David's cause have been forgotten.

The scene as he waits for news is drawn in poignant detail. The first messenger, Zadok's son, prevaricates though he already knows the tragic truth (18:20). The second messenger, eager for the anticipated reward, blurts out what he thinks to be good news for David. With dramatic irony the atmosphere changes. David's grief is unrestrained. His throne is safe, yet all is nothing to him weighed against Absalom's death. The father's love distorts his vision. The one rebellious son, root cause of the battle, is to him of more value than all his devoted men, hence the heart-rending words of 19:3: 'The troops stole into the city that day as soldiers steal in who are ashamed when they flee in battle.'

Joab challenges David's self-centred grief. He must show himself to the troops or risk being disowned (a challenge not unlike Disraeli's to the long-absent Queen Victoria, absorbed in her private grief).

Now that Absalom, their favoured king, is dead, the northerners (the kingdom of Israel) renew their allegiance to David. But David has still not learnt wisdom. He makes another foolish decision, wilfully stirring up rivalry between the north and his own southern tribe, Judah, provoking it into competition with the Israelites (v. 12).

Why Amasa is appointed to replace Joab as military commander (v. 13) is not clear. Joab had saved the day for David, rallying the disheartened troops. Was it personal revenge against Joab for the brutal murder of David's beloved Absalom, or cold political calculation to win the support of Amasa, who had been Absalom's general (17:25)? David is now undisputed king of both north and south. Yet the antagonism between them still goes deep (see vv. 41–43) and the fragile unity of the tribes would soon be reversed (20:1), a hint of the permanent schism which was to follow Solomon's death.

David's dilemmas were real. They may seem to us the outcome of uncontrolled, unwise emotions, even sometimes of spiteful revenge. But we, too, can face conflicting commitments and difficult decisions in our

Christian lives, as Jesus warned his first disciples (Matthew 10:37). What guiding principles can help us resolve such painful, and sometimes life-changing, dilemmas?

4 Mixed motives

2 Samuel 19:24—20:2

From start to finish, this has been a story of mixed motives and political intrigue. Of Mephibosheth's character, so far, we have known little. Saul's grandson, heir to his throne, hindered by physical disability from active resistance to David, has grovelled before David's generosity while, according to Ziba (16:3), secretly awaiting the opportunity to oust David from power.

In today's passage he emerges as a loyal, even noble figure. The details of his unkempt appearance are significant (v. 24). His is no opportunistic pretence of mourning for the absent king. The signs of his mourning are longstanding, and his excuse rings true. We need, then, to re-evaluate Ziba's accusation. It is the latter, not Mephibosheth, who is guilty of double-dealing. David's own suspicions are shown in the question he put to Ziba back in 16:2 and here to Mephibosheth (19:25). Mephibosheth's final words (v. 30) are noble, doubly so since Ziba had slandered him in 16:3. David's own motives are ambiguous. Is he acting from pure generosity or simply political calculation? It is refreshing to move from these complex motives to Barzillai's sincere devotion. Chimham, whose services he offers David (v. 37), was probably his son.

The story resonates with today's world in its shifting, uncertain allegiances. Even here there are glimpses of tensions between north and south: Judah whole-heartedly and Israel half-heartedly rally to the king (v. 40). But a jealous quarrel is brewing. Judah's relationship to David is the closer but Israel, with many more tribes, claims more 'shares' in the king (v. 43). Yet their loyalty is less certain than Judah's. By the end of our passage we find them ready to follow another leader, Sheba—a scoundrel (literally 'a man of Belial', 20:1–2). Sheba is a Benjaminite, a tribe eventually allied with Judah in the southern kingdom but at this period in an indeterminate position and originally Saul's tribe. The hosti-lity was deep-seated and the fragile unity soon reversed. Sadly, David himself was not blameless, deliberately provoking intertribal rivalry. Yet amid the welter of human emotions and the tangled mass of political intrigue and self-serving manipulation, God was working out his purposes. He is no less present today in our uncertain world.

5 The mighty Lord who hears and answers

2 Samuel 22:1–20

With relief we move from tales of brutality and subterfuge to this great psalm of thanksgiving for deliverance (with minor variations, found as Psalm 18). Of David's many enemies, only Saul is named, although he has played no part in 2 Samuel. The reference points back to 1 Samuel and Saul's bitter hostility to David. In many chapters we have found little overt reference to God and his purposes, but David, despite all his faults, knew where true deliverance lay—hence his heartfelt outpouring of thankfulness.

David's is no 'domesticated' God, merely a larger-than-life figure. He is the Almighty, awe-inspiring in majesty, veiled in darkness and mystery, yet glorious in dazzling light (vv. 12–13). Those dramatic forces of nature, thunderstorm and earthquake, hint at his awesome power, and this is the God who reaches down from heaven's heights to deliver and to save. His purposes are veiled in mystery, not at human disposal or human whim, yet he is always ready, even waiting, to hear our prayers.

The psalm draws on mythological language familiar in the ancient Near East: 'he rode on a cherub and flew' (v. 11). Forget modern depictions of cherubs! The cherubim of the Old Testament are glorious beings, overshadowing the mercy seat in the temple (Exodus 25:19, 21–22) and associated with God's chariot throne (Ezekiel 10:18–19). There is truly an element of terror in the portrayal of this awe-inspiring God.

Then comes the amazing contrast: 'he reached from on high… he drew me out of mighty waters' (v. 17). By its inclusion in the Psalter, this psalm has given expression in many centuries of Christian worship to those who have experienced divine deliverance. It is a reminder that, in the One who in extreme weakness and mortal suffering saved us, not from human enemies but from all the powers of darkness, God did indeed 'bend the heavens and come down'; he did indeed 'reach from on high' to save us. The magnificence of the psalm awakens our amazement and praise. 'From his [heavenly] temple he heard my voice' (v. 7), hearing, reaching down, saving—but there is more than that. In Jesus, the Lord did not simply reach down; he came and dwelt among us.

Read this psalm alongside the story of the incarnation in John 1 and let it lift up your heart in praise and worship.

6 David, repentant and generous

2 Samuel 24

We are brought down abruptly from the heights to confront the depths of reality. The psalm of praise is not the end of the book. Instead we have a strange and, for us, disturbing view of God. Angered by Israel, so the ancient writer tells us, God 'incited David against them' (v. 1). The Chronicler, retelling this incident several centuries later, felt the difficulty and attributed the incident to Satan, not the Lord (1 Chronicles 21:1).

Joab was reluctant to conduct a census of the people but his query went unanswered (v. 4). It was a vast undertaking, lasting nine months and more, covering north to south and territory beyond the Jordan. When the undertaking was complete, David was burdened with guilt. Why so? Why was a census regarded as so objectionable? The reason is unclear. Joab's response (v. 3) hints at excessive pride on the king's part. In earlier times, Moses had twice taken a census at Yahweh's direct command (Numbers 1:1–4; 26:2). The situation was different now, however, in the time of Israel's strength, united under the monarchy.

There was clearly more to the census than meets the eye. Its association with conscription, implied in verse 9, or possibly with taxation, seemed to threaten the liberty of the individual citizen. Certainly David knew that he had acted unlawfully.

Three alternatives were offered in retribution (v. 12). That troubles us. What kind of God is this? David sees it differently: 'Let us fall into the hand of the Lord, for his mercy is great' (v. 14). It is easy to accuse David of blatant selfishness, choosing suffering for the people in preference to personal suffering. Each penalty, however, would have involved the people. In fact, what he chooses is the affliction of least duration. With our individualistic attitudes we find it offensive that the people should suffer for the king's offence, but a little thought puts it into perspective. This is reality, and the world today is no different. How many terrible disasters are brought on nations, on the powerless masses, through the foolish or selfish actions of those in power? Today's headlines give too many frightful examples.

David acknowledges his guilt: 'I alone have sinned, and I alone have done wickedly; but these sheep, what have they done?' (v. 17). It is a prophet, Gad, who brings the word of the Lord to bear on the situation. Out of all the conflict and turmoil that have blighted this story, David's final words are spiritually perceptive and an uncomfortable challenge to us: 'I will not offer burnt-offerings to the Lord my God that cost me nothing' (v. 24).

The story ends abruptly. From the parallel account in Chronicles we learn that Araunah's threshing floor became the eventual site of the temple (1 Chronicles 21:28—22:1).

Guidelines

The Old Testament is clearly not a book of ready-made devotional thoughts. It is the history of a people struggling to survive in a brutal world, threatened by powerful nations and internally by political intrigue. It is a story marred by sickening destruction of human life and sometimes wanton cruelty, but in this is its relevance to our equally violent and fractured world. We read of the wavering loyalties of its leaders, whether to each other or to the Lord. Yet through it all, unseen and often ignored, in the long term God was in control, working out his purposes not by easy miracles but in the complex events of life. And the marvel is this, that out of that maelstrom eventually was born the gospel in the full mysterious glory of God's intervention in our world, a God who sees and cares—and saves.

FURTHER READING

R.P. Gordon, *1 & 2 Samuel* (Old Testament Guides), JSOT Press, 1984.

John Goldingay, *Men Behaving Badly*, Paternoster Press, 2000.

David M. Gunn, *The Story of King David: Genre and Interpretation*, JSOT Press, 1978.

DEAF THEOLOGY

As part of the growing interest in minority perspectives on theology and the Bible, there has been an increasing focus on the particular perspective of Deaf (and disabled) people. Previously, if they were represented in theology at all, it was within topics such as suffering or healing. However, the lives of Deaf and disabled people are much more than that: we can and do read the Bible from a particular viewpoint, and we bring insights, fresh perspectives and new ways of thinking that are not only relevant to us but to others as well.

I capitalise the word 'Deaf' to reflect the fact that many of us consider ourselves primarily a people who use a different language. When we are together in situations where everyone is using sign language, we do not consider ourselves impaired in any way. We are more than people who can't hear; we have a community and a culture of our own.

I will be writing about various passages that resonate with my life as a Deaf person who uses British Sign Language. It is not a definitive Deaf theology: there are many views of what it means to be deaf. It is one person's view, but I hope that all who read it may find something to touch their lives as well.

When I quote the Bible, I shall be using the New Revised Standard Version.

1 The infinite variety of God's creation

Genesis 1

British Sign Language (BSL) is a visual language, so, while it is as capable of communicating abstract philosophical discussion as any other language, it is in descriptive passages that it really comes into its own. Signing Genesis chapter 1, we build up a picture of the extraordinary richness and variety of God's creation. This passage describes all the different plants and trees and the variety in the swarms of living creatures. As any birdwatcher, botanist, zoologist or photographer would appreciate, there seems to be no limit to the possibilities for difference in God's creation: we can never reach the end and say that we have identified every possibility in existence.

This is true of theology as well. Even after 6000 years and counting, we've not yet said everything there is to say about God, and we never will. There is always something new to say, or a new way to express old truths. As more and more people from different backgrounds find their theological voice, even more variety is bought into theological reflection. Deaf people are one of the groups that have recently joined the great discussion about God, contributing a perspective rooted in our sign language, our Deaf culture and community, our predominantly visual perception of the world and our history of oppression.

So what is our reaction to the variety of God's world and talk about God? Do we constantly take refuge in the familiar? Or do we allow the differences to touch us and rejoice in each new species discovered, each new thought expressed? After all, the last verse of this chapter tells us that God saw everything he had made and, indeed, it was very good.

2 Who gives speech to mortals?

Exodus 4:10–12

When God called Moses to lead his people from Egypt to the promised land, Moses' initial reply was to say that he couldn't do it. In verse 10 he protests that he is 'slow of speech'. God's reply to Moses here has been at the heart of the survival of Deaf culture and sign language despite over 100 years of attempts to suppress them. The reply is, 'Who gives speech to mortals? Who makes them mute or deaf, seeing or blind? Is it not I, the Lord?' In the face of attempts to convince Deaf people that their sign language was inferior to speech and that they should instead try to act as much like hearing people as possible, Deaf people have quoted this passage to reply, 'We are as we are, made by God to be as we are and not to try to be like someone else.'

When I was a child and a teenager, as the only Deaf child in my school I felt like a second-class hearing person—always behind, always asking, 'What did they say?' When I discovered the idea that I had been created by God to be a first-class Deaf person, to be the 'me' I was uniquely created to be, it felt like liberation. Being Deaf still had its frustrations, but they no longer included the pressure to be what I thought I should be, rather than being who I was.

Trying to be something that is impossible for us to achieve is a source of much human stress and low self-esteem. It is good when we can learn to accept who God has created us to be, to accept the limits of our unique bodies and characters, and seek to develop what we are rather than striving after what we are not.

3 Trust in others, trust in God

Exodus 4:14–16

This passage from Exodus is a description of the very first interpreter. Moses claims to be slow of speech and tongue—which suggests that he has a speech impediment—and when he continues to protest that he can't do what the Lord is asking, the Lord concedes that Aaron can speak to the people on Moses' behalf, if Moses tells him what to say.

Deaf people have an interesting relationship with sign language interpreters. It is a relationship of trust: we have to be able to trust that the information signed to us accurately reflects what has been said and, if we sign in reply, we have to trust that the interpreter is accurately relaying what we want to say to the hearing person. The relationship relies on the interpreter's ability to subdue their own personality and thoughts and simply relay information from one person to another. It is also a relationship that provides the punchline to many jokes in the Deaf community as we seek to process our need to depend on another human being to quite that extent.

Sometimes people ask, 'Isn't it better to lipread? Then you won't be dependent on sign language interpreters.' But lipreading does not reduce dependency on others: it relies on the ability of the other person to make themselves easy to lipread.

Is dependency all bad? It is impossible for humans to be totally independent of others, but some of us really struggle with this fact. Yet we are called to learn to trust in God for everything, to acknowledge our total dependency on God for all that we are and have. Putting our trust in other people and learning to accept our dependency on them is a step to learning to live by trust in God alone.

4 Why me?

One of the great questions that all humans face at some point in their lives is 'Why me?' It is usually a question that emerges out of times of suffering. The history of Deaf people, as individuals and as a community, has its share of suffering. Deaf children have been rejected by their hearing parents and, in mainstream schools, have found themselves isolated and bullied. Sign language was once banned in residential schools because it was thought to interfere with a Deaf child's ability to learn speech, so children were caned if they were caught using it. Deaf women were sterilised so that they couldn't pass on their 'condition' to another generation—before it was realised that less than ten per cent of deafness has a genetic cause. Deaf adults have been restricted to menial employment, regardless of their talents, because others have had low expectations of their abilities. Deaf Christians have been discouraged from signing in church because sign was not considered to be a good enough language with which to talk to God.

This suffering is part of the history and experience of Deaf people. We need to acknowledge and cry aloud and lament and be angry: if we deny our experience and pretend everything is all right, we are not being honest with ourselves or with God. There is a long and honourable tradition of lament in the Bible. Many of the psalms were written as laments in the pain of exile. Psalm 22, for example, begins with the question, 'Why have you forsaken me?' Why leave me to suffer?

Christians are tempted to think that we must always be praising and thanking God and must not complain. Yet, by the glory of the Holy Spirit, we can move on from lament and anger to being able to give praise and thanksgiving from within suffering, because that is where we have met the living God.

5 Ephphatha: be opened

Mark 7:31–37

It is impossible to reflect on the Bible from a Deaf perspective without looking at this passage. Apart from anything else, this man is the only deaf character in the Bible. This being so, it is a shame that many Deaf people cannot in fact identify with him. Many, if not most, Deaf people do not consider themselves as 'sick' and in need of healing, if that means being made to hear. For some Deaf people, the idea that Jesus sees them only as someone to heal is a barrier to following Christ.

Over the years, Deaf theologians and preachers have developed four different ways of approaching this text. The first is to dismiss the man as obviously not culturally Deaf and therefore of no relevance to Deaf people today. The second is to say that just because this deaf individual needed to be made to hear, it doesn't mean that all deaf people need it: Jesus looks at people as individuals. Third, it is possible to focus on Jesus' use of sight and touch to communicate with the deaf man and therefore emphasise Jesus' desire to relate to him rather than to heal him. Finally, reading from a Deaf liberation perspective, it is possible to say that the healing received by the deaf man wasn't about being made to hear: what was 'opened' was not his ears but his heart to the saving love of Jesus. When he was made to speak, it wasn't the power of speech that was given to him but the confidence to tell others by sign what he now knew. The healing power of Jesus was an inner healing of the scars of low self-esteem, which kept him cowering in the corner.

Healing is a sensitive topic in Christian circles, but Deaf views on this passage suggest that we can never determine what form the healing of another, or indeed ourselves, can take. We need to be open to whatever God wants for us.

6 Jesus was helpless too

Luke 22:63–65

John Hull, in *In the Beginning There Was Darkness*, speaks about Jesus in this passage, when he was blindfolded and mocked with the words 'Prophesy! Who is it that struck you?' Hull writes of how much he and other blind people can identify with the ignorance and humiliation of Jesus in that moment, because of their own experiences of both intentional and unintended humiliation.

I can remember many incidents at school when children would run up to me, say something with their mouths hidden, and run off again while all around screamed with laughter. I guessed that they were insulting me or saying rude words of some sort, but I never did find out what they were saying. Even now, the potential for embarrassment, if not downright humiliation, is always there when I cannot understand what is being said to me, especially if the person concerned simply does not know that I am deaf.

Coming away from such situations with cheeks burning and emotions all churned up, it is comforting to know that Jesus knows exactly how I feel at that moment because he has been through it himself. Even the all-seeing, all-knowing Word of God has faced that experience of total helplessness. We are not told how Jesus reacted, but the implication is that he did not try to argue or fight back; he simply stood quietly until they had finished.

We all have times in our life when we face situations of humiliation and total helplessness. In such situations, we can end up raging at others, or we can judge that we deserve what is being done to us because we are blind or deaf (or old or young or whatever), thus reinforcing our own lack of self-worth.

But Jesus shows us another way. We certainly do not deserve such treatment, and we do not need to protest in anger either, when such protests often only exacerbate the teasing. We can choose to be quiet and dignified in the face of undeserved ill-treatment, holding on to the fact that our Lord has been this way before us and is there at our side.

Guidelines

This first group of reflections has focused on the experience of Deaf people as individuals in society, and on our experiences of difference and exclusion, of dependence and suffering. It is also an experience of the acceptance of self, of healing and liberation, and of meeting with the God of the Bible, the God who sides with the poor and suffering against the powerful.

It is impossible to separate out the positive and negative sides of being Deaf, or, indeed, of being human. Reflecting on these experiences in relation to scripture puts them into the perspective of God's relationship with the people of God; this leads to both a deeper appreciation of the Bible and a deeper understanding of the experiences.

I invite you to reflect on significant moments in your life in relation to scripture in the same way, and find the truth for yourselves that even a place of humiliation can become a place of rejoicing because that is where we have an encounter with Christ.

1 Go, make disciples

Matthew 28:16–20

At the end of Matthew's Gospel, Jesus instructs the eleven apostles to 'go therefore and make disciples of all nations'. This command has been obeyed to the extent that there are few, if any, nations of the world that have not had at least one missionary visiting them to proclaim the word of God.

Deaf people, too, have their missionaries—men like Matthew Robert Burns, a remarkable Deaf man from Edinburgh who, inspired by the 19th-century evangelical revival, set up the first known Deaf church in the UK in 1830. Now many towns and cities in the UK have their own Deaf church somewhere—and some have more than one. Deaf churches may meet in chapels based in Deaf centres or as separate congregations in the 'hearing churches'. Services in the Deaf church are conducted in BSL, perhaps with a voiceover for any hearing people who attend and cannot sign. There is a big difference between services conducted in BSL and services that are spoken and interpreted into BSL to make them accessible.

Holding services in BSL means that not only are the words of the service chosen with BSL in mind, but also that the culture of the service is the visual culture of Deaf people, and the context is the Deaf community. Language, culture and community come together to make the

Deaf church, at its best, a place where all Deaf people can participate in and lead worship, a place where all Deaf people can be active disciples of Christ.

When Jesus commanded the eleven to 'go… and make disciples', he wasn't just asking them to collect souls or keep up the numbers in church. He was commissioning them to call others to an active, living relationship with God, a relationship that makes those others in their turn want to go out and tell even more people the good news of Christ.

When we obey that call and reach out to those who are different from us because of their culture or age or for any other reason, we need to consider what we are calling them to. Are we asking them to try to copy our way of being Christians, of worshipping God, or are we open to the fact that they may accept God's call but want to find a different way of expressing it?

2 *Logos*: Jesus the Sign of God

John 1:1–18

One of the more confusing titles of Jesus in the Bible is 'the Word of God'. It's confusing not just because it is theologically dense, with many layers of meaning, but also because of its abstraction, which can cause difficulties in seeing how it can mean anything in a personal relationship with Christ. The Greek word translated as 'word' in this passage is *logos*: 'the divine principle of reason that gives order to the universe and links the human mind to the mind of God' (HarperCollins Study Bible, 1993). Another way of expressing *logos* is to say that it represents God's overwhelming desire to communicate with the people of God, a desire that reached its pinnacle when the Word became flesh and God's only Son was sent to live as one of us.

Many Deaf people today have grown up believing that to communicate with God, we need to do so in English: we need to speak. This belief originates from the time when sign language was suppressed in schools, after the Congress of Milan in 1880, partly because speech was seen as the 'light of the soul, and the soul on earth is the light of the divine idea' (M.G. McLoughlin, *A History of the Education of the Deaf in England*, 1987). There is still a belief, found in many of the Deaf churches, that SSE (Sign Supported English, a hybrid form of sign language that follows the English word order rather than the grammar of BSL) is the correct way to worship, the correct way to communicate with God. However, SSE, for many people, is hard to follow clearly and does not encourage Deaf people, who do not use it naturally, to communicate with God themselves in prayer. This experience does not fulfil God's deep desire to communicate with us in a language we can understand and, in fact, provides a barrier to such communication.

It is not just Deaf people who feel that to communicate with God, we need to do so in the 'proper words'. We all need to recognise the *logos* of God, the deep desire to communicate which means that God will pick up on all our unexpressed yearnings and most inarticulate grunts, whatever language we are using—whether signed or spoken or simply thought.

3 What is written in the law?

Luke 10:25–37

The Disability Discrimination Act (DDA) was passed in 1995, and further amended in 2005, making it illegal in the UK to discriminate against anyone on the grounds of disability: 'Failure or refusal to provide a service that is offered to other people to a disabled person is discrimination unless it can be justified.' Places of worship are included as specific examples of the everyday services to which disabled people, including Deaf people, should be able to expect access. For Deaf people, this means not only the provision (and use) of loop systems for those who benefit from them but also the provision of written copies of what is being said where possible, and Sign Language interpreters as well. The law asks for 'reasonable adjustments', recognising the different financial and material resources of different places, so there is no blanket minimum standard of what must be provided.

Obviously the law must be obeyed but, as Christians, do we only do what the law requires? Jesus poses the challenge of law-keeping to the lawyer in verse 26 before telling the parable of the good Samaritan, in which he suggests that our call to love our neighbour goes far beyond what the law requires.

What this means for us is that the DDA becomes a tool to enable us, as Christians, to further fulfil our call to love and serve our neighbour. It is not just our buildings but also our attitudes that can throw up barriers, making it difficult for Deaf people to access all that Christ offers through the church.

In addition to its five Deaf churches, Liverpool diocese has churches that are identified as 'Deaf friendly'. In some of these churches, sign language interpretation is provided on a regular basis; in others, support is provided for the Deaf person by someone who sits with them to make sure they are following the progress of the service. It doesn't matter what level of support is provided; the Deaf person is made to feel welcome and wanted and included in the life of that particular church.

Examining our attitude to our Deaf neighbour costs nothing. It can make all the difference, for a Deaf person, between feeling rejected—not just by the church but by the God the church represents—and feeling welcomed, loved and valued as God values them.

4 Will we be Deaf in heaven?

Revelation 7:9–12

This vision of people from many different places and speaking different languages, standing equally before the throne, brings to the fore a question that arises in Deaf theology from time to time: 'Will we still be Deaf in heaven?' There are several views on this question. Some say 'yes', arguing that the important parts of our identity—including being Deaf—will still be identifiable, but we will no longer be subject to the limits imposed by being Deaf. In other words, in heaven all people will know sign language as well as every other language, so there will be no barriers to communication. Other Deaf people struggle with the idea that they can be Deaf without limits, and argue that in heaven they will be able to hear.

This diversion of views arises from the perception held by both Deaf and hearing people that those who only have four working senses are somehow less human than those who have five—that Deaf people are, in fact, not equal to hearing people.

We humans have a tendency to rank people, including ourselves, in a hierarchy depending on the differences between us, implying that those who can do certain things better than us are somehow better people. In addition to judging five senses 'better' than four, we often consider those who are physically more attractive than us, or more intelligent, or who have more money, to be better than us.

However, the Bible makes it quite clear that this is not God's view of the matter at all. In addition to the picture of people of all tribes and languages standing equally before the throne, we are told in Galatians 3:28 that all are one in Christ Jesus. It is not only in heaven, where all barriers and human limitations are done away with, that we shall be equal, but also here on earth. If we can make our churches a place where all are equal, by valuing each other not for what we can do but for who we are, then our churches can become a preview of heaven on earth. Wouldn't it be wonderful, when we are asked what heaven is like, to be able to point to our churches and say, 'Come and see for yourself'?

5 Multisensory worship

Psalm 141

Seventy people, most of them Deaf, descended on Chester Cathedral recently for the day. We had an interpreted tour of the cathedral in the morning, followed by an act of worship in the afternoon. This act of worship was created and led by Deaf people and focused on the expression of Deaf culture in worship. Hearing people who joined the congregation found themselves moving and dancing to a sign language song in total silence at one point, even though they did not fully understand sign language. Afterwards, everyone, Deaf and hearing, felt that they had benefited from this worship, which had used the whole body and included all five senses. The Deaf people present (many of whom had not experienced worship in their own culture before) said they felt liberated!

Psalm 141, often used for the opening responses in evening prayer, says, 'Let my prayer be counted as incense before you, and the lifting up of my hands as an evening sacrifice' (v. 2). This is a reminder that worship in the Old Testament was a feast for the senses and the whole body, with the smell of incense and the movement of the arms in prayer, along with the sights and the sounds of the temple. It is also a reminder that worship is so much more than just the words we use and the songs we sing. We are embodied, sensory people: if worship does not deliberately engage all our senses and bodies, we will be taking in information through all our senses anyway. We don't switch off part of ourselves when we enter a church building. This does not mean that every act of worship should be 'smells and bells' or full of dancing and waving arms, simply that thought needs to be given in every church to what will be seen as well as heard, smelt and touched as well as sung, and enacted with our bodies as well as spoken with our mouths or hands.

6 Praise God!

Psalm 150

Psalm 150, the last psalm in the Bible, is a psalm of praise. It gives a sense of all the different instruments with which people used to praise God at the time it was written—a chaotic and glorious noise of trumpets, lutes and harps, tambourines, strings, pipes and, of course, the loud clashing cymbals. With its reference to dance (v. 4), we can imagine all the people dancing in wild abandon as the only way of expressing the fullness of their hearts when they think of the wonderful things that God has done.

It's a wonderful psalm but the references to the instruments are meaningless to a lot of Deaf people, so we have created our own version, recreating the scene as it might happen in a Deaf church, using symbolism of movement and visual stimuli to replace the sound of instruments. It is a valuable reminder that there is always more than one way to praise God!

Alleluia!
Praise the holy God.
Praise the Almighty God.
Praise God for everything he has done.
Praise God with big signs.
Praise God with lively dancing.
Praise God with hands that clap.

Praise God with waving flags.
Praise God with flashing lights.
Praise God with stamping feet.
Everybody come and praise the Lord.
Alleluia!

PSALM 150 (DEAF WAY) © HANNAH LEWIS 2002

Guidelines

In this second week of looking at Deaf perspectives, we have focused more on the experience of Deaf people in the church and as a worshipping community. This hasn't just been about what the church can do for Deaf people, but also about what Deaf people can offer the church. It is worth finishing this week by reflecting on how we can indeed be the multifaceted body of Christ that the church is called to be—a place where the gifts of all are recognised and used, and differences and variety are celebrated as a reflection of the multifaceted nature of God.

FURTHER READING

On theology and deaf people:

Hannah Lewis, *Deaf Liberation Theology*, Ashgate, 2007.

Wayne Morris, *Theology without Words*, Ashgate, 2008.

On theology and disability:

John Hull, *In the Beginning There Was Darkness*, SCM, 2001.

Nancy Eiesland, *The Disabled God*, Abingdon Press, 1994.

THE DARK SIDE OF GOD

There are a number of passages in the Old Testament that present a rather difficult view of God. They portray him as acting unjustly, capriciously, even violently towards righteous people. How do we reconcile these pictures with those of a more compassionate and loving God, or even with the God of justice and might so often portrayed in the Old Testament? How can human beings have faith in a God who asks more than is reasonable of his servants, who subjects them to tests of virtue? How far can human beings interact with God and ask him to change his mind? Is God really working on Israel's behalf when he threatens violence against them in his anger? These questions and more are raised by the passages I have gathered together for this week of readings. We need to confront the difficult texts alongside the more palatable ones in order to get a fuller picture of God and of his, at times, uneasy relationships with his servants.

This aspect of God, in fact, reflects human relationships, which would be unnatural if they were always easy. Made in the image of God, we humans often have a 'dark side' which we struggle with and try to offset. We need also to confront this aspect of the Old Testament, which causes many people to avoid engaging with its pages.

The version of the Bible used is the Revised Standard Version.

2–8 NOVEMBER

1 What about the righteous?

Genesis 18:16–33

If God always rewarded the righteous and punished sinners according to a strict principle of retribution, we would all know where we stand! This doctrine appears often in the Old Testament (in Deuteronomy and Proverbs most overtly) and clearly works some of the time, perhaps most of the time, but not all of the time—and that is where the problem arises.

In this passage, God is about to destroy a whole city, indiscriminately.

A contrast can be seen near the beginning of the passage between Abraham, father of the chosen race, who is instructed and expected to 'keep the way of the Lord' by his righteous and just behaviour (v. 19), and Sodom, a city outside the chosen nation, whose sin is 'very grave' (v. 20). Yet the presupposition seems to be that God judges all peoples according to the same principles, whether they are inside or outside the chosen race.

Abraham dares to challenge God on the issue of righteousness: the problem with wholesale destruction is that 'fifty righteous' may be caught up in it. Is it right to punish all, when only the majority have sinned? Abraham appeals to God's essentially just dealings, rebuking him directly with the famous phrase 'Shall not the Judge of all the earth do what is just?' (v. 25, NRSV). There is a conflict here between God's power and justice. Because he is all-powerful, God can do what he likes, but to interact with human beings he needs to conform to a shared sense of justice.

This is a risky strategy on Abraham's part, given God's propensity for anger (v. 32), but the risk pays off. The challenge causes God to change his mind and show his compassionate side: he declares that he will forgive the whole city for the sake of 'fifty righteous' (v. 26). We might think this, too, is unjust! The wicked will have 'got away with it'—yet arguably God would be giving them another chance.

Abraham treads carefully as he reduces the number of 'righteous' who might save the city to ten (v. 32). We could ask the question: would just one innocent person have saved it? We hear the outcome of the debate, though, in Genesis 19, where God destroys Sodom after all—but only because there are no righteous inhabitants left, Lot and his family having been taken out.

2 The ultimate sacrifice?

Genesis 22:1–14

Here Abraham is subject to what J.L. Crenshaw calls 'a monstrous test' (*Whirlpool of Torment*, p. 9). God has enabled Abraham and Sarah to conceive a son in their old age, and now Abraham is being asked to sacrifice that same son to the Lord. What kind of God asks this kind of sacrifice of his righteous servants? Does it betray a cruel streak?

The text gives no hint that Abraham might object or disobey. We hear the trusting and bewildered words of the boy, 'Where is the lamb for a burnt offering?' (v. 7), and the pious response of Abraham that the Lord will provide (v. 8). Abraham is at the point of brandishing the knife when the sacrifice is called off. But why was it commanded in the first place? Was it to convince God of Abraham's total obedience? This is indicated in the text when the angel says, 'Now I know that you fear God' (v. 12). But didn't God know that already?

The ram is found and used as a substitute, but we are left with an unsavoury feeling that God has behaved in an unnecessarily cruel way. Imagine the feelings going through Abraham's mind—those that are not found in the text—as he tries to pluck up the courage to stab his own son with a knife and then to subject his body to burning on the altar of sacrifice. As any who are parents will know, the action doesn't bear thinking about. Is it right that God should test his faithful servants in this way? Is it meant to be character-building? If so, it seems a strange way to achieve the aim. Giving a cruel command and nullifying it at the last moment can be seen, at best, as an act of great fickleness on God's part. And what about Isaac, the innocent victim? A mere boy who had done nothing wrong could have lost his life at the hand of a person he trusted, his own father. As R.N. Whybray writes, 'However important the story may have been in the mind of its author as a proof of Abraham's unwavering and unquestioning faith and trust in God's purposes, the callous deception practised by God and his indifference to human suffering cannot have failed to impress the original readers' ('Shall not the Judge of all the earth do what is just?', p. 7).

3 Change your mind, God!

Exodus 32:1–14

If anything would be designed to provoke God's anger, it's the incident of the golden calf, in which, while Moses' back is turned, the Israelites make and worship an idol—probably symbolising Baal, the Canaanite god of thunder who was often represented by a bull—out of their gold jewellery. In some sense, however, God gets carried away by his anger, threatening to 'consume them' in his wrath. Here, again, God has the power to effect wholesale destruction, and he displays a 'fierce wrath' that is almost irrational. Moses is the only one who is exempt, and God wishes to make him the new founder of a dynasty (v. 10).

Yet Moses implores God to change his mind in the light of the fact that the Israelites are his chosen people. What is the point, he asks, of the great deliverance from Egypt if God is just going to 'consume them from the face of the earth' (v. 12)? What will the Egyptians think when they hear about this destruction? The implication is that God has a reputation to maintain among foreigners as well as Israel—even among his enemies. Moses appeals also to the great patriarchs of the past and God's great promises of descendants and land (v. 13).

Again, God is shown to listen to his faithful servant's daring rebuke and change his mind. His ultimately compassionate nature takes over from his darker side—even though the people certainly deserved to be punished for their wrongdoing.

There is a similar passage in Numbers 14:13–20, where Moses again intercedes for the people, reminding God of his reputation with the Egyptians and that he has promised to be 'slow to anger, and abounding in steadfast love, forgiving iniquity and transgression' (see Exodus 34:6–7a). This is an appeal to God's 'better nature', which is in conflict with his dark, angry side.

4 Death of a good king

2 Kings 23:21–30

The books of Kings present a history of the kingship in Israel, with the deeds of good and bad kings alike. Unfortunately the bad ones seem to proliferate, and the temptations of idol worship, wizardry, soothsaying and augury are too great. At last, in 2 Kings 22, we find a good king, Josiah, who is God-fearing, casts out idols from the temple and effects real reform, bringing in a new regime of law-keeping. In our passage he has just ordered a Passover to the Lord, a practice which had died out but which is prescribed by God in the 'book of the covenant' (v. 21: thought to be what is now Deuteronomy).

Josiah is the hero of the Deuteronomistic history: 'Before him there was no king like him, who turned to the Lord with all his heart, with all his soul' (v. 25). This is praise indeed—higher even than that given to David, founder of the dynasty. In verse 26, however, we are told that God is still angry with the nation because of the bad kings, such as Manasseh (see ch. 21).

Can guilt be inherited from one generation by another? Ezekiel says 'No', in his discussion of individual responsibility (Ezekiel 18). Here, however, God resolves to destroy Judah and Jerusalem for Manasseh's sin, just as he has formerly destroyed Israel, the northern kingdom (v. 27). Sin appears to be cumulative. Josiah himself, as the nation's representative, becomes the victim of this judgment, being killed in battle by Pharaoh Neco, king of Egypt (v. 29). We might wonder what God is doing, allowing one of the best kings to be cut off in his prime: he was a mere 39 years of age. Of course, the king who followed him began the slide into sin once again, and so the bright light was extinguished.

Is this how God treats his most faithful servants? An innocent man, who behaved in a righteous manner all of his life, is prematurely killed, so what has happened to the system of just reward? Whybray writes, 'Josiah's death is clearly intended to be understood as a particular act of God that was not only unjust but was a personal and national tragedy that hastened the demise of the kingdom of Judah' (p. 12).

5 In order to horrify them!

Ezekiel 20:1–26

Ezekiel is writing from exile, trying to interpret the situation theologically. Chapter 20 gives a bleak picture of Israel's history, expressing the prophet's view that right from the start, even before the monarchy, the Israelites had misbehaved such that punishment was inevitable. He sees history as cyclical: at every step the people misbehaved and at each point God 'thought I would pour out my wrath upon them' but stopped himself 'for the sake of my name' (vv. 8–9, 13–14, 21–22). Here the picture is not of a God of compassion but of one who is anxious about his reputation in the sight of the nations. Yet God's consistency is emphasised, with an inference that if he wants to be in relationship with his people and the wider world, he needs to show forbearance.

However, when we get to the last generation, it is as if God's patience is running out. In verse 25, instead of giving his people good ordinances and every opportunity to behave righteously, we read that the Lord deliberately gave them 'statutes that were not good and ordinances by which they could not live'. It seems that God is playing a trick on this generation, deliberately leading them astray as a punishment. Verse 26 continues that God made them 'offer by fire all their firstborn'—a reversal of the Passover rescue—in order 'that I might horrify them… that they might know that I am the Lord'. God is deliberately betraying his people as a punishment for ongoing sin. Perhaps his attempt to 'horrify' them is meant to shake them into submission, but it sounds a bit like Abraham's test and doesn't portray God in a positive light. The law is usually seen as a good thing in the Old Testament, sent to enable righteousness, not to hinder it, but here the very goodness of that law is laid open to question.

While there is evidence of some early legitimate sacrifice of the firstborn (see Exodus 22:29–30), the practice was not widely followed and was found to be increasingly distasteful. Perhaps this is what the prophet is alluding to in verse 26, taking the opportunity to express his evaluation of its true purpose—God's attempt to 'horrify' his people.

6 God's wager

Job 1—2

The book of Job presents another test from God to a man who couldn't be more righteous (1:1). When God holds Job up to Satan as an example of pious behaviour (v. 8), Satan challenges God, suggesting that Job is righteous for the sake of reward: material prosperity, social status, longevity, many descendants and so on. Is it right that God should allow this righteous person to be made subject to a heinous test—the result of a heavenly wager—that destroys his family, his property and virtually his sanity? This test goes even further than the testing of Abraham, as the destruction is not forestalled.

Job's reaction to his losses is to abase himself in the posture of mourning (v. 20). His response is that since he came into the world naked and expects to die naked, anything given to him in between is a blessing from God and so God should be praised.

When Satan is then permitted by God to inflict Job with a terrible skin disease, again Job's mood is one of acceptance (2:10), expressing the view that we have to accept good and evil from God, even if we don't understand why they happen. This suggests that God can do whatever he likes and that principles of justice and retribution are simply not operative. Job knows that he has not sinned, so why else would he suddenly be treated by God in this way? He knows nothing of the wager in heaven.

The Job who starts to speak at the beginning of chapter 3 is much more lamenting and protesting of his fate. Perhaps his lament is more realistic in the light of the great suffering that has befallen him. But the question is still raised: what is God doing, subjecting his servant to a test that leaves him desperate, and giving him no answers? Even at the end of the book, in the speeches of God from the whirlwind (chs. 38—41), there is more said about God's power in creation than about his justice in terms that human beings can understand. God appears to act in total freedom and cannot be pinned down by human understanding. While this tells us something about the omnipotence and power of God, it does raise worrying questions about his justice towards us.

Guidelines

Many people flounder in their faith, faced with the problem of the suffering of the innocent. We have to ask: what kind of God metes out wholesale suffering to communities and even nations in natural disasters, and to individuals who have led a good life who don't appear to deserve that suffering at all? Despite Abraham's protestations about Sodom, many places are destroyed by fire, flood and earthquake with no regard for innocent, God-fearing people. A pious person like Job, afflicted with disease, reminds us of the many we know who are struck down by cancer, often at a young age. Then there are accidents that involve sudden death or horrific, life-changing injuries.

We can take some of the blame as human beings: if we drive around in fast cars, aren't accidents inevitable? If we choose to build a house on a flood plain, don't we get what we deserve when flooding occurs? And yet, if we believe in a God who is on our side, who doesn't wish to see us suffer—indeed, in one who suffers alongside us—how can he allow such things to happen? Are we experiencing God's 'dark side'? Are we forced to take any idea of justice out of the equation and see good and bad in the world as essentially matters of chance?

There are more questions than answers to these issues. The passages we have looked at show that the Israelites were well aware of the problem of how to reconcile righteousness with punishment. Job provides perhaps the most profound answer to suffering: it is ultimately an encounter with God and a sense of God's overwhelming power and higher purposes that leads Job to realize his own smallness. We can, as humans, be guilty of trying to force God into a mould or pattern that suits us but also belittles him. Maybe God's justice is greater than ours. However, it does seem that he listens to us, and, if Abraham and Moses managed to challenge him to change his mind, maybe he will do the same in our lives.

FURTHER READING

J.L. Crenshaw, *A Whirlpool of Torment: Israelite Traditions of God as an Oppressive Presence* (Overtures to Biblical Theology 12), Fortress Press, 1984.

R. Davidson, *The Courage to Doubt*, SCM, 1983.

R.N. Whybray, 'Shall not the Judge of all the earth do what is just?': God's oppression of the innocent in the Old Testament', in D. Penchansky and P.L. Redditt (eds.), *Shall Not the Judge of All the Earth Do What Is Right?: Studies on the Nature of God in Tribute to James L. Crenshaw*, Eisenbrauns, 2000.

J.L. Crenshaw, *Defending God: Biblical Responses to the Problem of Evil*, OUP USA, 2005.

WALKING THE PSALMS: A JOURNEY OF MENTAL HEALTH

The Psalms contain a rich tapestry of human emotion, from the amazing highs of the wonder of the God who created everything to utter lows of bitterness, loss and exile. Brought together over many centuries, they tell the story of people and their relationship with God, in poetry of the human soul laid bare before all who would look on. The emotive force contained in these texts provides a powerful lens through which to survey the landscape of mental health in our society, in which depression appears to have reached epidemic proportions and the search for happiness is relentless.

I hope that the next two weeks will provide some insight into the journey of mental health. However, as I issue the invitation to you to walk with me for a while, I must confess that I am not an armchair explorer of this territory. In April 2003 I finally succumbed or submitted (I still haven't decided) to the reality of the dark cave I had entered and a diagnosis of depression, which has more recently been recognised as a condition called Cyclothymia. This does not mean I am less of a person than I once was; I am still amazed by the stigma that surrounds the diagnosis of a mental health condition, especially within churches. I enjoy a full, active and busy life as a priest, academic, writer and husband. It is simply that sometimes my family and friends need to hold me tighter, forgive me my weakness and remind me of the God who will never abandon me.

So walk with me a while, bear with my passion and honesty, and perhaps discover for yourself the God who never abandons us but leads us into glorious new days.

Two of the sections are written by my wife, Tamsin, to give her perspective on my journey.

Quotations are taken from the New International Version of the Bible.

1 The journey begins

Psalm 142

We are told in the title of this psalm that we are to picture David in the cave of Adullam (see 1 Samuel 22:1; 24:3), a reminder of his treatment at the hands of the increasingly troubled Saul, who was undergoing his own trauma. Crying out to the Lord, pouring out his complaint, telling the Lord of his troubled heart, and faint of spirit, David looks around and sees that no one is concerned for him; no one cares for his life. He has entered the cave and is isolated from the illuminating warmth of daylight and from the companionship that might have restored to him the hope of another tomorrow.

David's story has so far been one of remarkable triumph: we are told, 'Whatever Saul sent him to do, David did it so successfully that Saul gave him a high rank in the army' (1 Samuel 18:5). When we meet David in Psalm 142, we are left wondering what has happened to this successful champion of the battlefield. How has he come to be lain so low that he would declare, 'Listen to my cry, for I am in desperate need; rescue me from those who pursue me, for they are too strong for me' (v. 6)?

In my own mental health journey, I found that the moment of crisis was not when the edifice of my pretence of normality crumbled; rather, it was the point when I realised I had entered the cave. There was no light and I was alone. Alone in the cave, you cry out and the only sound that reverberates from the walls confirms the pain of your own loneliness. Yet in the echoing chamber of isolation there is a choice to be made: the darkness may surround but, outside the cave, the sun still shines and the warmth of friendship can still be experienced.

The power of Psalm 142 is the cry of David's heart, mind and spirit, troubled in his isolation, calling to the Lord, whom no cave can hold: 'Set me free from my prison, that I may praise your name' (v. 7). The challenge that David sets for us is the challenge of hope—the hope that things will change, that there is a way out of the cave, and that at the end of that journey there is the light of a new day where companionship waits.

2 Knowing despair

The depth of pain expressed in Psalm 137 is extraordinary. Resonant with the bitterness of exile and loss, it builds to a climax containing the darkness of absolute despair. There is little comfort in this psalm. There are no platitudes to stir the warm fuzzy feeling of shallow faith, which dares not face the torment of the world, lest it wither. Psalm 137 is about the lived experience of pain and a reminder that despair can fuel hatred in a furnace that would desire the deaths of a generation of children. Walter Brueggemann writes, 'It is not for us to "justify" such a prayer in the Bible… it is not one of the noble moments of the Bible, but it is there.'

Despair can hold us prisoner as our soul rages at the world's cruelty to us. It can cause us to harm those who try to comfort us, and we consider ourselves alone and unwanted. However, it is not an exile imposed upon us, but one in which we are the journeying ones. Psalm 137 does not represent a people taken from their homes without warning. For decades the Lord had been calling his people back to his ways, and then they found themselves separated from all that was familiar, sitting by the shores of an unfamiliar river as captives.

Depression turns people in on themselves, stealing character, bringing exile from familiarity and opening up despair. It is a journey I have travelled myself, and the danger is in staying beside the river, imprisoned by the despair of hope lost and life afflicted. The psalm asks, 'How can we sing the songs of the Lord while in a foreign land?' (v. 4). I believe the answer is, 'Because we must not forget.' In the exile brought about by a mental health crisis, we forget the place we have travelled from. We forget the time of laughter, love and enjoyment, and happiness becomes a memory, difficult to grasp. We need companions who will bear our pain, endure our anger and, as they sit alongside us by that unfamiliar river, sing songs of remembrance and hope, songs that remind us of who we are.

3 Being a friend

A psalm probably used in the context of a special service as the king and his army prepared for battle, Psalm 20 provides us with an outline of intercessory prayer (vv. 1–6), declaration (v. 7) and praise (vv. 8–9). As you read the words, you can imagine the priests before the assembled army, preparing for a difficult battle as they face the sophisticated warfare of chariots and horses (v. 7). Therefore, words of blessing and declaration are spoken over those who face the challenge ahead, who will experience the blood and loss of battle, reminding all who hear to 'trust in the name of the Lord our God'.

I've entitled this section 'Being a friend' as I have found that those who stand beside me, who declare God's blessings over me and remind me to trust in the name of Lord, even when my mind is in the darkness of the difficult battle ahead, are friends who know the Lord and who know me.

The scene involving the priests and army was a picture not of 'them and us' but of the people of God gathered together as one to pray for the time ahead. Being a friend to someone facing mental health difficulties is to stand alongside them for the battle to come and declare that, before the Lord, we are one. This kind of friendship says that we stand and fall together, and it is costly. The easier response is one of separation, to see yourself as different from the person with depression, bipolar disorder or similar condition. But the Levitical priests knew that their status was by accident of birth: if they had been born within a different tribe, they would be the people marching out into battle. They knew that their identity and fate were entwined with all the Lord's people: there was no 'them and us'.

Research into mental health has identified the effect of genetic heritage. Whether or not we will face the battle of mental health can be determined by our genetic make-up, in which we have no choice. To be a friend is to be someone who understands that 'there but for the grace of God' goes each one of us on our life journey. To stand alongside will be costly but, without one another, we are less than we could be and weaker for the battle ahead.

4 'Where are you?'

Psalm 22 opens with an echo across the centuries: 'My God, my God, why have you forsaken me?' The question takes us to the scene of Christ's crucifixion, as the same words were spoken out before those who looked upon the death of the Messiah. Whenever I read the words, they tear at me. The sense of an utter break in relationship and isolation—'Why are you so far from saving me?'—takes me to the dark place of the cave and the coldness of separation. How Christ endured that separation upon the cross is a mystery that I do not want to understand, for as I edge my way towards it I am reminded of the darkness and separation that depression can hold.

It is in that place of darkness that the mind turns inwards to consume what little light exists for the soul. 'I am a worm, not a human being' (v. 6) is the stripping of confidence and self-worth; 'All who see me mock me' (v. 7) is the power of paranoia, fed by a mind that constantly whispers, 'They hate you; you are hateful', until the soul is stripped bare and agony is all that seems to exist for the one who suffers.

However, Psalm 22 provides a powerful three-letter challenge for the one who is suffering: 'Yet…'. This is the point at which the psalmist stops floundering in his grief and starts to find his strength: 'Yet you brought me out of the womb; you made me feel secure' (v. 9). The power of 'yet' is to recognise that, in the midst of the darkness of despair, mine is the choice to endure and survive. It reminds me of the garden of Gethsemane, before the crucifixion, where Jesus faced the reality of forsakenness and prayed, 'My Father, if it is possible, may this cup be taken from me. Yet not as I will, but as you will' (Matthew 26:39b).

In a mental health crisis, hope is an elusive and illusory concept, but 'yet' is a sliver of light that penetrates to reveal what might be, would be, could be. If 'yet' is embraced, we discover that the world can pivot on the tiniest moment to reveal the light of renewed hope as we see the Father's love, which is not subject to the weakness of a mind but stands in the strength of eternity. 'Posterity will serve him; future generations will be told about the Lord' (v. 30).

5 Walking in shadow

Psalm 23

Derek Kidner writes of Psalm 23, 'Its contentment is not complacency: there is readiness to face deep darkness and imminent attack.' To walk in the valley of the shadow of death (v. 4) is to know the presence of death, an experience common to the mental health sufferer. Suicide, for some people, is a clear act to end their life, coming from a strong desire for death. For many people, the combination of self-destructive emotion, thought and behaviour, compounded by mental health problems, results in an increased desire to escape what they feel is overwhelming them, thereby increasing their risk of committing suicide.

I have lived with suicide and have taken the funeral of someone who decided to end their own life; I have witnessed the utter destructiveness of the act upon those who continue to live. Living with the desire for death is to walk through the valley of shadow, constantly aware of the mountainous threat that surrounds. This is when the shepherd's presence is vital. For me, the shepherd's presence is in my wife and friends, who allow me to talk about how I feel without attaching fear or stigma. Through them I see that I need not fear the presence of death, and in them I experience the goodness and love that follow me. Therefore, I find that I can understand David's psalm: there is no complacency but a contentment to live. There is no need to hide the darkness or threat from others, but in its place comes a need to acknowledge the presence of darkness and continue my journey of life.

Talking, openness, and a support list of friends and organisations who can cope with hearing someone they love talk about death are vital in protecting life. The shepherd of David's time led his sheep and the sheep knew his voice. He led them through the valley of death into the green pastures and quiet waters. In my life, the valley is never continuous but I know what it is to enter and walk its bitter length. Yet I also know what it is to hear the echo of the shepherd's voice from those prepared to walk with me, leading me to the place where the valley ends, the horizon opens and, for a while, my soul can be restored.

6 Remember what God has done

Psalm 103

(*Tamsin*) Psalm 103 reminds us of the God we love and in whom we put our trust. Verses 1–2 cry out to us to praise God and not to forget what he has done; when we do this, we share in the whole of God's story. Recently I had the privilege of taking part in a Passover meal with some students, and one thing that struck me was the way the Passover story becomes their story today. This is not ancient history; it is their history, to be told as something tangible. So I stand not just in God's saving action on my life but in the whole history of God.

Verses 3–19 remind us of all that the Lord has done, is doing and will continue to do. He redeems our life from the pit and brings justice for the oppressed. These words have great meaning for me, as those who suffer with mental illness are some of the silent oppressed of our world. The words remind me that although I love Rob, God made him and loves him more than I ever could. If I want him to be free, how much more does God?

A big challenge in the psalm comes in verse 8: 'The Lord is compassionate and gracious, slow to anger, abounding in love.' This will be a challenge for any of us who lives with someone else. We are to ask the question, 'How does God want me to change to love this person more?' rather than pleading, 'Oh God, please change them.'

It's tempting, as someone who is quite emotionally stable, to think that I can be Rob's rock. But—and it is a big but—verses 17–19 remind me that it is God who is *our* rock. It's not that I am Rob's rock, but that God is *our* rock. Psalm 103 is important as it reminds us to praise our Father in heaven, who loves us so much that he removes all our transgressions from us. He is the one who saves us, walks with us and forgives us as we blunder around. It is God's love that is everlasting, not mine; we are mere mortals, not gods, and let's not pretend otherwise.

Guidelines

(*Tamsin*) Living with someone whose emotions are up and down, you arrive home not knowing what emotion the person you love will be experiencing. I have found marriage to be a place of profound learning about the 'other', his perspective and troubles, trials and struggles, his joys, loves and passions. God made each one of us unique, and in marriage it's my privilege to get to know that 'other' in a deep and intimate way. So I may long for Rob to be free, but not as much as God does, for God longs for all of us to be free, so much that he died to set us free. But the true nature of God is not to gloss over our troubles but to come into the depths of our pain and darkness and walk with us through them.

My challenge is to ask the questions, 'How can I love and live with this person in the way the Lord would? What in me provokes difficulties for

Rob?' Recently I came home from work thinking, 'Whoopee! let's go to the cinema or out for dinner', but I'd come home to a husband with a 'bad head' (our phrase for the times when Rob's head has its own storm raging inside). I sank and thought, 'Oh, woe is me; we never get to go out'— which is an exaggeration. However, if I desire to live and love like the Lord, who is slow to anger and abounding in love, I need to find a better way to communicate. Rob does not want to be defeated by his head. So we talked, and we worked out that in future I could come home and say, 'I've had an idea. Would you take ten minutes to think about going out to see a film?' Rob would then take on the responsibility to think the suggestion through. Being an extravert who thinks out loud, this is not easy for me. I've had to learn to think and to ask myself, 'How do I need to phrase what I'm going to say, so that Rob has time to process it?'

When living with someone with depression, the challenge is not to allow hope or opportunity to be lost, but to reach out to love the person as God sees them and be prepared to be changed.

1 It doesn't last for ever

Psalm 30

One of the greatest falsehoods spoken by the mind in the midst of depression is that nothing is going to change, that darkness is all there is. However, this psalm is a song of restoration. The exuberance of David's joy, as he recognises God's enduring goodness towards him, leaps from the text: 'Sing to the Lord, you saints of his; praise his holy name' (v. 4).

David opens the psalm with the declaration, 'I will exalt you, Lord, for you lifted me out of the depths.' Commentators note that the latter phrase is literally, 'You have drawn me out…' which may be used for the drawing of a bucket from a well. Lifted from the depths into the light of day, David bursts forth, acknowledging healing and rescue from the pit.

For many people, depression is not a permanent condition. Winston Churchill famously described his 'black dog days', when darkness would overwhelm, but the days pass and treatment can draw the person up from the depths of the cold, dank well into the light of a glorious new day. It is wonderful when that day comes, when the black dog has bounded away, when you can feel the warmth of relationship and emotion once again. But it is surprisingly easy to forget the journey of being drawn out.

I find the image of the bucket a helpful metaphor to explore my experience of being drawn up out of the well. Cyclothymia is a condition in which I experience the despair of descent and the abiding joy of ascent. I try not to see the days spent deep in the well as useless but to draw up the water of the well within me. This does not mean holding on to the darkness, but being able to contrast it with the hope of a new day, so that I might rejoice all the more in the goodness of the one who draws me out. It is when we know such contrasts of life experience, as did David, that we understand David's acclamation, 'You turned my wailing into dancing; you removed my sackcloth and clothed me with joy, that my heart may sing to you and not be silent. O Lord my God, I will give you thanks for ever' (vv. 11–12). Amen and Amen.

2 'Lift up your head'

Psalm 24

This majestic psalm is one to read aloud, hearing the words resound their declaration, 'The earth is the Lord's, and everything in it, the world, and all who live in it' (v. 1), as you begin a journey to ascend the hill of the Lord, seeking his face to receive a blessing from the Lord. The spoken word is powerful; the sound of our voice can draw us out of ourselves and be wonderful when shaped by such glorious words of praise. The psalm tells us that only those who have clean hands and a pure heart, who have not lifted their soul to a false idol or sworn by what is false, may approach (v. 4). But good news! In Christ Jesus, the way has been made open for all who trust in his mercy to approach the Lord and receive blessing. In the midst of depression, such words can be difficult to speak aloud as you feel so utterly devoid of worthiness. Yet in Christ our worth is not determined by how we feel but by his redemptive grace poured out upon us.

When I was at university, someone said to me, 'Lift up your head; you're the son of a king!' I cringed at the time when I heard this, but in recent years the call to 'lift up my head' has been a constant reminder of the physicality of depression. Hunched over, you walk along not daring to look up and meet anyone's gaze as you simply try to survive the journey. Some years ago, John Stott wrote the following story:

I read… of a young man who found a five-dollar bill on the street and who from then on never lifted his eyes when walking. In the course of years he accumulated 29,516 buttons, 54,172 pins, 12 cents, a bent back and a miserly disposition. But think what he lost. He could not see the radiance of the sunlight, the sheen of the stars, the smile on the face of his friends or the blossoms of the spring time.
From *Declare His Glory among the Nations* (ed. D.M. Howard, IVP, 1977, p. 90)

So lift up your head and see that the King of glory approaches, 'the Lord strong and mighty, the Lord mighty in battle' (v. 8). Know that you are a child of the King of glory: look up, see the sun shine, the stars glisten, the clouds move upon the breeze, and know that you are greatly loved.

3 'Why are you downcast, O my soul?'

Psalm 42

I talk to myself. When I'm feeling particularly down, I talk out how I am feeling and acknowledge what is happening inside. Psalm 42 brings us into a conversation of the heart where the individual is talking to himself. Most commentators agree that Psalms 42 and 43 should be interpreted as a single psalm of lament. Lament is a powerful form of expression in scripture as it recognises how our experience of life can be disconnected from our experience of God. There is a mismatch that takes place, and God appears to have forgotten us. Walter Brueggemann observes, 'Psalms of darkness may be judged by the world to be acts of unfaith and failure, but for the trusting community, their use is an act of bold faith… because it insists that the world must be experienced as it really is and not in some pretend way' (*The Message of Psalms*, Augsburg, 1984, p. 52)

The expression of our experience of darkness through lament is supported by research that demonstrates the benefit of bringing out into the light of day how we are feeling, what we are experiencing and the questions we might be facing. My mode of expression is through writing; yours might be through painting, pottery, carpentry, cookery—in fact, any number of creative outlets. The power of expression is to reveal what is stored up inside the mind and soul, even if it is shocking to those who pretend that the world isn't really as bad as the reality of your experience. In doing so, we acknowledge that 'deep calls to deep in the roar of your waterfalls; all your waves and breakers have swept over me' (v. 7).

However, there is a need to develop Brueggemann's 'trusting community', in which these expressions of lament can be heard and shared. Too often, the person experiencing the darkness of mental pain is silenced through the inability of others to bear the bold act of lament. Lament is not about shame but about expressing pain and, in doing so, discovering hope. If we silence lament, we silence hope: 'Why are you downcast, O my soul? Why so disturbed within me? Put your hope in God, for I will yet praise him, my Saviour and my God' (vv. 5, 11).

4 Nowhere to run

Psalm 139

Psalm 139 is a psalm of realism. 'O Lord, you have searched me and you know me' (v. 1) is a statement that is both vivid and sure in its description of the reality of God's presence. Yet, for the psalmist, God's closeness, familiarity and knowledge of his ways almost proves too much and the impulse to flee is considered. But where can he flee in order to escape God? The heavens, the depths, the darkness: none of them can hide us from the one who knit us together in the womb.

When I was first diagnosed with depression in April 2003, I fled to seek somewhere I could be alone, only to discover that I already was. I took out my mobile phone to call someone, anyone, to try to reconnect with friends, but I realised that I hadn't spoken to many of them for over a year. It was not the fault of my friends. I had retreated into my mind to maintain the outward appearance of normality and had been separating myself from anyone who might have seen what was truly happening. I fled to the depths and to the darkness and God was still there; his was not always a welcome presence to me, but God was still there.

Someone once described depression to me as a thief: it is only after you discover that you have lost your friends, your character and your hope that you realise you've been mugged. It can create a bitterness of regret and pity that can consume us. The lesson of the psalmist, however, is about zeal. In the sudden outburst of verse 19, the psalmist aligns himself with God, opposing all those who would deny God, and ends with a call to be searched and tested. In his zeal, the psalmist moves beyond the focus upon 'I' and declares the reality of 'You'.

Sometimes, in the midst of loneliness, we need to be reminded of the reality of God's presence, the 'You' with us. He does not leave us or deny us, but knows our innermost being, our souls stripped bare. Even when he has looked upon the nakedness of our heart, he still holds us as precious and known. No wonder the psalmist offers himself to be searched and tested, when we can trust so completely the one who looks upon us.

5 A new song of praise

Psalm 40

Psalm 40, ascribed to David, contains many echoes. Verses 6–7 find later reflection in Hebrews 10:5–7, and the prayer of verse 17 is later repeated in Psalm 70:5, but the heart of the psalm is a story of rescue and glad response. Verses 1–3 describe patience, the means of rescue, and a response. They are verses that continually speak to me of my own journey. David is at the bottom of a slimy pit, his feet stuck down in the mud and mire. There is no way he is going to climb out of the hole in which he finds himself. If he jumps about, trying to escape, he will only sink deeper into the mud and exhaust himself through his impossible task. So David waits, patiently, and calls out to the Lord, who hears his cry, comes and lifts him out, and sets David's feet on solid ground.

My mental health condition is cyclical, with down times and up times. I have learnt that in the down times, when I know I'm stuck in the mire, I must not jump about or surrender to sinking desperation, but need to be patient and wait. There will come a time when the down time passes and I know what it is to be lifted out, to be able to see the bright light of day and the horizon surrounding me. It is then that I understand why David describes 'a new song' in his mouth, 'a hymn of praise to our God' (v. 3): solid ground feels great when you have been up to your knees in mud.

Patient waiting does not mean the denial of a situation. Later in the psalm, David asks God not to withhold mercy but to protect him, acknowledging that troubles surround him that are more than the hairs on his head (vv. 11–12). There is honest reality in David's patience: perhaps, even when he is in the pit, he knows that his rescuer will come to lift him out. This is what I have learnt in my own patient waiting, that I can cry out and be honest about my feelings and situation, but rescue does come, and when it arrives it is glorious and praiseworthy: 'The Lord be exalted!'

6 Choosing to smile

Psalm 150

Psalm 150 closes the whole Psalter with an extraordinary burst of exuberance. Derek Kidner observes that these six verses contain the where (v. 1), why (v. 2), how (vv. 3–5) and who (v. 6) of praise. The call to worship is the recognition of God as God: 'the compassionate and gracious God, slow to anger, abounding in love' (Exodus 34:6). There are times when I find the exuberance of worship difficult. The numbing of antidepressant medication, combined with unreliable emotional resources, does not make for a great worshipping experience. However, I have discovered that at times I am called upon to offer a sacrifice of praise. I saw such a sacrifice for the first time when a close friend led his church in worship shortly after discovering that his beloved grandfather had died. He had tears of loss rolling down his face but still he sang of God's goodness. My friend chose to acknowledge God in his mighty heavens, praising him for his acts of surpassing greatness. His choice to praise has always remained with me.

The idea of choice in the midst of mental health crises is not a popular one. As a patient, you and your emotions are medicalised, your brain chemistry is altered and you are provided with a variety of therapeutic interventions, some of which you are told about only after the event. You are disempowered, and to have someone speak about 'choice' in the midst of that disempowerment is not always welcome.

However, the choice I speak of is about my responsibility to acknowledge God's goodness, power and greatness through praise, even when it is the last thing I want to do. It is my responsibility because I know God and God knows me. I cannot deny that relationship, which sustains, rescues, upholds and enfolds me in compassion and grace. It is at this point that the psalms burst into power for me. When my own emotions are unreliable and my ability to praise is numbed, I can take hold of these extraordinary words of reality and hope and express my whole self in them. 'Let everything that has breath praise the Lord. Praise the Lord' (v. 6).

Guidelines

I once heard a psychologist describe his flight to attend a conference. The airport was overcast, clouds pouring down rain, suppressing the light. The plane took off through the storm. Passing through the clouds, all visibility outside disappeared and the aircraft was buffeted by the swirling air. Then it happened: the plane burst through the clouds and into a glorious blue sky and bright, wonderful sunshine. The psychologist realised that the storm clouds may gather and seem to drive away the light, but above the clouds the sun still shines. The storm will pass, the clear blue sky will be seen again and the warmth of the sunshine will be felt once more.

I have carried that story close to me over the last few years. It reminds me that regardless of the storms that seem to blot out my view of God, the Son continues to shine his glorious radiance, the day still contains light, the storm will cease, and a new day of hope will come to warm my soul.

If you travel with mental health needs, hold on to the truth that the storm will pass and a new day will come. Allow friends to speak words of hope over you as you seek to survive and live. Nothing can separate you from the love of God that is in Jesus Christ our Lord, so hold on to the reality of that truth when all else seems to fade.

If you serve or love a person with a mental health need, hold on to the story of who they are. Do not despise them for their words or feelings and do not pity. Instead, walk with them, hold them when they stumble, carry them when they fall, follow when they run away from you, and forgive when you are pushed away. In truth, yours is the greater journey with the harder calling—to love someone who cannot love themselves.

But in all these things we are more than conquerors through him who loves us. Why are we conquerors? Because we live to see the Son rise and the heavens break forth.

FURTHER INFORMATION

www.mind.org.uk   www.papyrus-uk.org

www.samaritans.org.uk   www.crusebereavementcare.org.uk

2 KINGS

Reading chapter 1 of 2 Kings illustrates the artificiality not only of verse and chapter divisions but also, in this case, of book divisions. The narrative barely pauses for breath between the end of 1 Kings and the beginning of 2 Kings: at the end of 1 Kings (which *Guidelines* explored in the previous issue), Ahaziah, the son of the infamous Ahab, had ascended to the throne after the death of his father and ruled in the northern kingdom, while the beginning of 2 Kings recounts a fatal injury that he received and the events that took place before his death.

Whereas the focus of 1 Kings was Solomon and the aftermath of the split between the northern and southern kingdoms, 2 Kings focuses on the kingdoms' fast-approaching demise. Throughout the book it becomes increasingly clear that God's people, both in the north and in the south, are rushing towards destruction: their unwillingness to listen to the prophetic voices around them, their attraction to the worship of other gods and their seeming inability to walk in the way of the Lord all combine to point to a single gloomy outcome.

Woven into the gloom, however, are threads of light. 2 Kings tells the story not only of those who failed to follow God's command but also of those who were faithful. We read of prophets, like Elisha, and kings, like Josiah, who struggled against all odds to do as God asked of them. As we read, it becomes clear that the final editors of this book (often called the Deuteronomistic historians because of the book's affinity with the book of Deuteronomy) told stories which they hoped would change the world in which they lived. Many scholars agree that these books reached their final form either during the exile or immediately after it, and that they aimed to provide a message of hope to the people. They told the story of how the exiles had reached their current state so that they might mend their ways, return to God and ultimately, also, return to the land that God had given them. 2 Kings is intended to be a transformative book, not just telling gloomy history for the sake of it but encouraging its readers to change.

Readers will notice that the passages chosen from 2 Kings focus on the first nine and the last ten chapters. The book is too long to be able to explore it thoroughly in three weeks. Consequently I have decided to focus on the most significant sections: the first nine chapters feature the ministry of the great prophet Elisha and the downfall of the house of Ahab; the final ten describe the events leading up to the destruction of the two kingdoms. Both sections give us something of the flavour of the whole book and help us to understand what the authors were trying to achieve as they wrote.

1 Is there no God in Israel?

2 Kings 1

This first chapter of 2 Kings paints a vivid picture of the current state of affairs in the northern kingdom. King Ahaziah is injured and seeks divine guidance for the future but instead of seeking this guidance from the Lord God of Israel, his own land, he sends messengers to the god of Ekron for wisdom. This presents, in a nutshell, the issues for the northern kingdom. Ahaziah was the grandson of King Omri, the founder of the infamous Omride dynasty, whose most hated son was Ahab (Omri's son and Ahaziah's father). The significance of Ahaziah's actions here is that, as king, he should have maintained and represented to the nation a particularly close relationship with God; instead, at a time of great crisis he sends messengers to Philistia, the ancient enemy of his people, to enquire about his recovery.

The name Baal-zebub in Hebrew is slightly unclear. The Greek translation of the Bible renders it as 'Lord of the flies' (from which William Golding derived the name of his famous novel), but Hebrew specialists are not agreed about whether this is the correct translation of the word. One of the problems is that Baal is a Canaanite god but Ekron, the place to which the messengers are sent, is a Philistine city. One possible way to explain this confusion is to point to the mutual influence that existed between the Philistines and the Canaanites. The other is to acknowledge that 'Baal-zebub' is simply a pejorative phrase used to show the futility of the king's actions: he was prepared even to ask the Lord of the flies before he enquired of the Lord.

If anything, it is the king's response to Elijah that best illustrates the extent of the situation in the northern kingdom. Rather than repenting of his actions, Ahaziah sends successive military units to kill Elijah for his criticism. For each of the first two times, the units are consumed by fire (which reminds us of Elijah's great victory on Mount Carmel against the prophets of Baal), and on the third occasion Elijah, saved from slaughter by the captain's fear, sends the same message again to the king, who then dies as Elijah had prophesied. This vignette of the terrible state of relationship between the Omride dynasty and God and his prophets sets the scene as we turn our attention to the next episode in the history of God's people.

2 The spirit of Elijah rests on Elisha

2 Kings 2:1–18

One of the only redeeming features of the reign of Ahab was the prophetic ministry of Elijah. The counterbalance to Ahab's determined apostasy was the courageous resistance of Elijah, who, despite the danger to his life, pointed constantly towards what God required. In chapter 1, which we explored in the previous reading, the continued need for Elijah's prophetic resistance during the reign of Ahab's son, Ahaziah, became all too apparent. The end of Elijah's ministry therefore marks a potential crisis: what will happen when Elijah no longer prophesies? The answer to this question is provided as Elisha picks up Elijah's cloak, or mantle. So significant is this event that the phrase 'to take up the mantle' has entered our language, meaning to carry on in the steps of another with similar actions and words.

This succession narrative finds a parallel in only one other story of the Old Testament: that of the succession of Joshua to Moses. Josephus, the Jewish historian writing at the end of the first century AD, drew strong comparisons between the succession of Joshua and that of Elisha. Two characteristics in particular are worthy of note. In both cases the successor not only accompanied his master to the end of his ministry but also undertook a very similar role after his master's ministry had ended. The striking difference between the two, however, is that while Moses died and was buried, Elijah was taken up to heaven in a fiery chariot, where he dwelt without dying. This spectacular end to Elijah's ministry ensured that his influence far outstretched his original lifespan. In both Jewish and Christian tradition, Elijah is regarded as a second Moses (drawing yet another connection between Elijah and Elisha, and Moses and Joshua) who will precede the Messiah when he comes.

This tradition can be seen most clearly in Malachi 4:4–6, which reads, 'Remember the teaching of my servant Moses, the statutes and ordinances that I commanded him at Horeb for all Israel. Lo, I will send you the prophet Elijah before the great and terrible day of the Lord comes. He will turn the hearts of parents to their children and the hearts of children to their parents, so that I will not come and strike the land with a curse.' It is also picked up in Gospel traditions about John the Baptist and the transfiguration (see, for example, Matthew 17:3–13).

3 The Shunammite's son

2 Kings 4:8–37

Elisha's ministry opens with a series of stories about his miracles, which are similar to but even more awe-inspiring than Elijah's. He makes an undrinkable spring of water drinkable once more (2:19–22), two bears maul 42 boys who insult him (2:23–25), he causes miraculous water to flow so that the Moabites are fooled into thinking that the Israelites are defeated (ch. 3), and he makes a poor widow's oil jar produce large quantities of oil (4:1–7). The episode in 4:8–37 is yet another example of Elisha's miraculous ability.

One of the important features of these stories is that they illustrate that Elisha, the great prophet, cares equally for matters of state and for individuals. Elisha's help in defeating the Moabites immediately precedes the account of his care for the destitute widow of one of his colleagues. Elisha is a prophet in Israel who, like God himself, cares about the people from the greatest to the least.

This particular story has two parts to it: Elisha's desire to give the precious gift of a son to the Shunammite woman who has cared for him, and his desperate attempt to revive the son after he dies. One of the most affective elements of the story is the grief of the woman at the death of her son and her reminder to Elisha that she did not ask for the son in the first place. The implication is that she would have been much better off never to have had a son at all than to have one and lose him.

Many commentators point out the slightly fumbling attempts of Elisha to heal the boy: first Gehazi, Elisha's servant, holds a staff over the boy's face, then Elisha lies down on the boy mouth to mouth, and finally bends over the child a third time. The impact of this threefold action to heal the boy is to imply anxiety and concern on the part of Elisha. He is reluctant to give up until the boy is healed. In this concern for the woman and her son, we see that Elisha is no glamorous wandering healer, only concerned for his own reputation, but a prophet who illustrates God's care for his people by his actions. From villages who struggled to survive, to the king in battle, to a destitute widow, to a wealthy woman who has everything but a longed-for child, God—in the person of his prophet Elisha—cares and intervenes for their welfare.

4 Naaman

2 Kings 5

The story of Naaman takes the story of Elisha one step further. So far we have encountered stories of people within Israel who were cared for by Elisha. The story of Naaman takes us, literally, into new territory: Syria. Syria, otherwise known as Aram, was an ancient and almost constant enemy of the Israelites, engaging in regular warfare with them. The fact that Naaman can travel into Israel alone points to the fact that this event must have taken place during a rare lull in hostilities; nevertheless, the point remains that God will heal even the most hated enemy of Israel who is in need.

Just as, in the previous story about the Shunammite woman, we could hear her loss and grief speaking between the lines of the text, here we meet the deep anxiety and desperation of Naaman. Naaman, we are told, was 'a great man' (v. 1; interestingly, the same word in Hebrew is used to describe the Shunammite woman in 4:8, yet the NRSV translates it there as 'wealthy'). However, he was eventually persuaded, despite his deep disgust, to bathe in the river Jordan—which, to give him his due, can be very muddy and unappealing in parts. The great Naaman must have been desperate indeed to be prepared to stoop so low to find healing.

Another feature that this story highlights is the fact that although Elisha's miracles were spectacular, he achieved them by unspectacular methods. He used salt to cleanse the water of the village (2:19–22), simply lay over the Shunammite woman's son to heal him (4:34), and here heals Naaman from afar by means of the muddy river Jordan. These miracles demonstrate God's power, not Elisha's.

This point is emphasised by the actions and fate of Gehazi, Elisha's servant, who sought to profit from the healing of Naaman. Gehazi demonstrated by his actions that he did not comprehend even as much as Naaman did. Naaman recognised that there truly was 'a prophet in Israel'—someone to whom God spoke—and thus acknowledged something of God's power in the world, whereas all Gehazi could see was what he might gain from that power.

5 The siege and the Syrians

2 Kings 6:30—7:20

The remarkable humility of Naaman, the Syrian commander, is cast into even greater relief in this story where the familiar warfare between Syria (or Aram) and Israel breaks out one more time. This story makes sense only in the light of the previous events (if you have the time, read 6:8–29), in which Elisha himself comes under threat from the Syrians when they discover that he is reporting all their movements to the king of Israel. What is important here is that Elisha decides that it would not be ethical to kill the Syrians because they were not captured in battle, and so lets them go. At the end of chapter 6 we encounter the vehemence of the Israelite king's wrath when he realises that they are now under siege and likely to die as a result of Elisha's leniency.

One of the striking features of this story is the way in which Elisha hides behind a closed door (6:32) because of his fear of the king. This reminds us of a theme that runs all the way through the stories of both Elijah and Elisha: although they are great prophets, they still cower in fear when the king or queen seeks their life (compare Elijah in 1 Kings 19, who ran away to the desert to escape Jezebel) because their power lies not with themselves but with God, and they are as vulnerable to punishment as anyone else. We should not suppose for a moment that these great prophets followed God's call without immense personal cost.

The theme is emphasised in chapter 7, which ends this episode. Despite the panic of the king and Elisha (6:32–33) and the cynicism of the captain (7:2), God assures the people that they will be saved from the Syrians. The discovery of their salvation is, notably, achieved by four lepers (resonances of Naaman in chapter 5), whose status as outcasts leads them to decide that they would be better off with the Syrians than with the Israelites. The denouement of the story is that the cynical captain who failed to believe God's word is trampled in the people's rush to find food in the Syrian camp (7:20).

6 Jehu and the death of Jezebel

2 Kings 9

The closing chapter of this part of 2 Kings (and of this week's study) is the final downfall of the hated house of Omri, as symbolised by the death of Jezebel, the widow of King Ahab. Although it makes today's reading a little long, it is important to read the whole chapter in order to get a sense of what is going on. The chapter opens in the reign of King Joram of Israel (the grandson of Omri and son of Ahab). This whole account is made even more confusing than usual by the fact that the king of Judah at the time was Ahaziah, who had the same name as Joram's predecessor and was, in fact, Joram's nephew, since Ahaziah of Judah's mother was Athaliah, the daughter of Ahab.

This chapter tells the account of Jehu's anointing by one of the band of prophets who travelled with Elisha, and his commission to destroy Ahab's descendants in revenge for what Jezebel had done to God's own prophets. Indeed, alongside the anointing of Jehu came a prophecy that Jezebel would also die, and not only that, but she would be eaten by dogs and not be buried. This was significant since in this period a 'good death' was considered to be one in which someone died at a ripe old age and was buried with their ancestors, leaving behind children to bear their name. Jezebel was to die before her time, to have no burial, and to have the rest of her family killed as well. The punishment for her many crimes in life was to be given to her at her death.

This final chapter in the story of the battle between God and the house of Omri, in particular Ahab and his hated wife Jezebel, draws together many of the themes of the rest of the story, most notably that what God promises will happen in all its detail. This chapter goes to great lengths to show how the prophecy made to Jehu at the start of chapter 9 is fulfilled at its end.

Guidelines

The story of the house of Omri, especially its most infamous son, Ahab, and his wife, Jezebel, tells in microcosm the story of God's people as a whole. Ahab and Jezebel symbolise how easy it is to be distracted from the worship of God. Their story began so simply. Jezebel was the daughter of a neighbouring kingdom, married to Ahab to establish a bond between them. In doing so, however, she brought into Israel the superficially more attractive worship of Baal, which led Ahab and many of his compatriots to turn from God and take up Baal worship. In contrast, the story of Elijah and Elisha shows those who battled against the odds—but entirely in God's power—to remind the people of God and to draw them back to him again.

Although the people and events are long past, there remain factors that draw people away from and towards God. Today the things that draw us away from God are very different, and are sometimes less obvious than in Ahab's day. Nevertheless, God still calls us all to be faithful and to proclaim the wonder of God's love into situations where such love seems alien and unwanted.

1 The evil of Ahaz

2 Kings 16

We pick up the story again approximately 100 years later, during the reign of King Ahaz of Judah. In the intervening chapters (10—15), atten- tion moved almost evenly between the northern and southern kingdoms. Now the attention shifts more firmly to the south. One of the reasons for this is that another great prophet has arisen who, though active during the reign of Ahaz, is not mentioned in 2 Kings until the reign of Hezekiah in chapter 19. This prophet, Isaiah, was one of the greatest the kingdoms had ever known and is remembered in our Bibles not just in 2 Kings but also in the book of prophecy named after him. It is this that draws our attention to the different perceptions in Judaism and Christianity of the book we are studying: Judaism associates it with the former prophets, while Christianity calls it Kings. In reality it is both—the story of kings and prophets, and of their bumpy journey together.

The particular story that lies behind this chapter is told again in Isaiah 7:1–25, a context that gave rise to the famous prophecy about a young woman bearing a child and calling him Immanuel (see v. 14). This was one of the most tense moments in Judah's history since, in the intervening years between the end of chapter 9 and the beginning of chapter 16, the Assyrian empire had grown and grown in power, so that now both Israel and Judah were its vassals, and had to pay extensive dues to the Assyrians to ensure peace. The reign of Ahaz saw an attempt between the ancient rivals Syria (Aram) and Israel (the northern kingdom) to rebel against Assyria and to persuade Ahaz and Judah to join them. Contrary to Isaiah's advice in Isaiah 7:4 ('Take heed, be quiet, do not fear, and do not let your heart be faint because of these two smouldering stumps of firebrands'), Ahaz sent to Assyria for help against Israel and Syria, with disastrous consequences: Damascus was destroyed. More importantly, Judah was forced to build an exact replica of the Damascus altar and to move the Lord's altar in the Jerusalem temple in order to install it. Ahaz had learnt no lessons at all from Ahab: Ahab's anxiety for the security of the nation caused him to marry unwisely and to destroy the nation from within, and Ahaz did the same.

2 The destruction of the northern kingdom

2 Kings 17:1–23

If the effects of Ahaz's action were disastrous for the southern kingdom, they were catastrophic for the northern kingdom. Although it is unclear whether Ahaz's call to Assyria for help against his northern neighbours was directly responsible for the destruction of the northern kingdom, it certainly cannot have helped. Nevertheless, the Deuteronomistic historians are clear that the ones ultimately responsible for this disaster were the people of the northern kingdom themselves. In case we had overlooked this fact, the authors remind us again of the sin of the people: their worshipping of other gods (v. 7), their adoption of other people's customs (v. 8) and their building of altars to other gods (vv. 9–12).

It becomes clear that the long, gruesome story that began back in the book of Joshua with the people's settling in the land is coming close to its climax—or at least in part. The story of God's people until now has emphasised two things—that such behaviour calls down God's punishment and that God's prophecies are always fulfilled. It was only a matter of time before this ending came about. Given its importance in the story, it comes as something of a surprise that the fall of the northern kingdom is covered in such brief detail, with only six verses of narrative (vv. 1–6) and 17 verses of comment (vv. 7–23). It becomes clear, though, that this is not in fact the climax of the whole story, merely a blip on the way to the climax.

In the minds of the Deuteronomistic historians, the destruction of the northern kingdom, catastrophic though it be, is yet one more step along the road to ruin but also, more importantly, one more chance for Judah to turn back and avoid that ruin. The people reading this story from exile were to take note that, time and time again, the people were warned of the disaster to come but they took no notice and continued as they were.

This passage points out that the fate of the northern kingdom was grim. The Assyrians mixed up the population so that some stayed in the land and were joined by people of other nationalities, while others were taken to other parts of the Assyrian empire. This story marks the end of the northern kingdom. The long, often unhappy history of the two king-doms, north and south, joined by a shared heritage and belief in God but pulled apart by rivalry and dissent, has now come to an end. As verse 18 puts it rather starkly, 'None was left but the tribe of Judah alone.'

3 Faithfulness to the Lord or to the Assyrians?

2 Kings 18:1–8, 13–18

If we were in any doubt about the message of 2 Kings, chapters 18 and 19 make it very clear. Hezekiah, Ahaz's son and successor in Judah, came to the throne and immediately demonstrated his loyalty to God by removing all the places of worship to other gods in the land. This, however, was not and could not be solely a religious decision. Ahaz's loyalty to his human overlords led him to build an altar to their gods; Hezekiah's loyalty to God caused him to break with the Assyrians and refuse to serve them (v. 7). The choice then became stark: God or the Assyrians? Divine or human authority?

The effect of Hezekiah's decision was felt, if not swiftly (the text suggests that he was in the third year of his reign when he made these changes and in the 14th year when retribution arrived), then decisively. The feared Assyrian army, under the leadership of Sennacherib, came to wreak retribution for Hezekiah's actions. Hezekiah's fear, recorded in verse 14, is a sign of how deeply the destruction of the northern kingdom had been felt in the south.

Hezekiah immediately repented and sent a message to the Assyrians, acknowledging that he was wrong and sending the wealth of the temple by means of a tribute. His following of God, then, was short-lived. Although he did what he thought was right at first, the fear of retribution caused him to change his mind entirely.

This is no superficial, facile message of faithfulness to God but a clearsighted understanding of the choices that have to be made: following God, right though it be, will not please human authorities. As Hezekiah discovered, the choice to follow God can bring with it hard human decisions.

Hezekiah, at least at this point in the story, demonstrated that his faithfulness was only skin deep. He was prepared to follow God, but only so far. If his loyalty to God conflicted with earthly, political decisions, then he backed down and instead sacrificed the things of the temple to his human overlords. Hezekiah's heart might have been in the right place but he found it hard to remain faithful when circumstances became difficult for him. It seems that he did not want to make hard decisions and hoped he could choose both God and the Assyrians. As events unfold, it becomes all too clear that this cannot be the case: he must choose one or the other.

3 On whom will you rely?

2 Kings 18:19–25; 19:14–19

The words of the Rabshakeh, an Assyrian army official sent to challenge Hezekiah, reinforce the choice to be made by Hezekiah. The Rabshakeh challenges Hezekiah to declare upon whom he can rely now that he has broken with the Assyrians (18:20). The human power of the Judean nation is so weak that they have no hope of resisting the Assyrians.

Hezekiah's distress at this message (19:1) indicates that he shares the Rabshakeh's analysis that all is now lost. The turning point of the story comes in 19:5–7, when Isaiah reminds Hezekiah that there is, in fact, another player in the fate of Judah, whom both the Rabshakeh and Hezekiah have overlooked. God himself is someone upon Hezekiah can rely.

Hezekiah's moving prayer in verses 14–19 calls upon God to act and come to the aid of his people. Alone, the Judeans have no hope of salvation, but with God on their side everything looks different. Hezekiah began his reign in the right way by dedicating himself to returning the land to the worship of God (see 18:1–8) but forgot one vital point: we do not have to act entirely on our own. Hezekiah sought to make everything right on his own and forgot that the covenant is two-directional. God calls us to worship but also binds himself to be our God.

A couple of historical points are worthy of note here. First, there is the question of whether or not these accounts are in the correct order. It seems odd that Hezekiah strips the temple to send tribute to the Assyrians (18:13–18) but there is no mention of this from the Rabshakeh when he comes out to challenge Hezekiah. Some scholars suggest that the events recorded in this section of 2 Kings are, in effect, two different episodes—one in which trouble is averted by the paying of tribute and the other in which the Assyrians come and besiege the city. Others argue that these events do follow each other and that the revenge of the Assyrians was to be expected, whether or not the tribute was paid.

The second issue concerns the account itself. It is striking to notice that this event is recorded verbatim in Isaiah 36:4—38:8 (which overlaps exactly with 2 Kings 18:19—20:11). This indicates how important this story was to the compilers of 2 Kings and Isaiah, but also that the story probably existed in a written form before it was used in either book (or was copied by one from the other).

However it reached its final form as we now have it, the message of this story is clear: Hezekiah sought to worship God but forgot that God understands this in terms of a relationship. God wants not to be a passive recipient of worship but to be part of a close and reciprocal relationship marked by heartfelt prayer and divine response.

4 The Lord intervenes

2 Kings 19:32–37

It will come as no surprise to readers who have become familiar with the message of 2 Kings that Hezekiah's prayer was answered by God and the Assyrians were defeated. Just as the Deuteronomists told the story of the long, slow decline of the northern kingdom from cherished nation of God to a country governed by those more concerned with personal gain and easy success, in order to show the inevitable outcome of ignoring God, so also they tell this story to affirm what can happen when people return to God. The end of the story is the answer to the Rabshakeh's taunt in 18:20: 'On whom do you now rely?' The response is, of course, upon God, who is a better ally and overlord than the Assyrians can ever be.

The events surrounding the Assyrian withdrawal are, surprisingly for Old Testament history, well documented outside the Bible. The authors of 2 Kings attribute the defeat to the slaughter of a large number of troops by the angel of the Lord; Herodotus, a Greek historian, says that the Assyrian army withdrew because a plague of mice went out and chewed their bow strings (*Histories* 2, 141) and, disappointingly in comparison to the drama of the other accounts, the Assyrian annals report an insurrection in Assyria, meaning that a major withdrawal of the army was necessary to go and sort it out.

Whichever account is relied upon, the effect was the same: the Assyrians withdrew from Judah at a time when the Judeans most needed them to, and at a time when Hezekiah had entreated the Lord to help them. It is hardly surprising that the Greek and Assyrian sources give less supernatural explanations for this surprising turn of events than do the authors of 2 Kings.

Interestingly, however, this salvation seems to have had a negative rather than positive impact on Judah's mindset. Scattered throughout the writings of the prophets are allusions to what scholars call the 'divine inviolability of Judah', which means that the Judeans believed that God would always save them because they were so special—not because Hezekiah had, for once, turned to God for help.

Indeed, it is a sad manifestation of human arrogance that we so often assume that we deserve the gracious, generous self-giving of God (and are indignant when we feel it has been withheld from us) rather than giving thanks for all we are given, whether we deserve it or not.

5 Not in my lifetime

2 Kings 20:12–19

Like many Old Testament characters, Hezekiah was flawed, with a complex mix of good and bad instincts. Immediately after the story of the dramatic and miraculous rescue of the city of Jerusalem, 2 Kings tells of Hezekiah's illness, in which Hezekiah insists on a complex sign—that a shadow should move back ten steps—as proof that he will get well again. Evidently the miraculous rescue of a city full of people was an insufficient sign of God's power and willingness to save. It is easy to criticise from a distance but Hezekiah's attitude is one that many of us find ourselves taking: 'Yes, I know God did that… but how do I know he can do this?' Throughout 2 Kings, the Deuteronomistic historians are seeking to push us to the answer that we know that God can and will do this because God has done so over and over again.

This particular passage of 2 Kings contains what is, at first glance, a shocking response by Hezekiah. After the fear of the Assyrian army had receded, another nation came to visit Hezekiah—the Babylonians—and Hezekiah showed them everything that Judah possessed in its storerooms. The heavy irony is that Hezekiah shows them everything that they will, in fact, take away in chapter 25, when they come to destroy the nation and remove all its wealth to Babylon.

Isaiah himself pointed this out to Hezekiah, to which Hezekiah responded, 'Why not, if there will be peace and security in my days?' (20:19). This response is troubling. How could Hezekiah accept so easily and so happily that his descendants would be annihilated when he himself was so distressed by the threat of the Assyrians only two chapters previously? The answer, when we think about it, is all too easy, because we all do it. It is very hard to feel the same level of distress over something we cannot or do not see as over something we ourselves experience.

We can't help wondering what might have happened if Hezekiah had railed against the prophecy, argued and expostulated with God? What would have happened if he had pleaded with God to change his mind? Of course we will never know, but Hezekiah's apparently blasé and selfish response rings hauntingly in our ears as the nation slides onwards towards destruction.

Guidelines

The theme that we have observed rumbling behind most of 1 and 2 Kings gets clearer and clearer as the story rolls on. This particular section of 2 Kings poses a simple question: 'On whom will you rely?' The choice is straightforward: choose God or the apparently powerful earthly rulers. It seems that many of Judah's kings tried hard to choose both but, as Ahaz discovered, it was impossible. Absolute loyalty to the Assyrians included worshipping at their altars; absolute loyalty to God involved eschewing anything that did not come from him.

It might appear that the Deuteronomists' message is simplistic in the extreme: trust God and all will be fine. In fact, though, it has more nuance than that. The story of Hezekiah acknowledges that relying on God is not without its problems. Hezekiah's turning to God did not prevent the Assyrians from besieging Judah, nor indeed from destroying a number of its major towns. Reliance on God is about long-term, not short-term benefit, and ultimately should be done because God is God and the others are not.

In some ways, the message of 2 Kings feels far distant from many of us. We are not facing the power of a mighty army or the fear of annihilation if we make the wrong choices. Nevertheless, 2 Kings contains a powerful and relevant message for each one of us, which is that seemingly innocuous choices about what we do and whom we follow can have enormous consequences. 2 Kings challenges us to think deeply about who and what we rely on and whether it is these people and things rather than our faith in God that call forth our loyalty and allegiance. The Rabshakeh's question is one that resonates down the centuries: 'On whom do you now rely?'

1 The evil of Manasseh

2 Kings 21:1–17

Whatever glimmers of hope for the future of Judah were raised by Hezekiah's tentative, though often shaky, loyalty to God are all wiped out during the reign of Manasseh. Manasseh was to Judah what Ahab was to Israel. Manasseh's evil was so great that even the immense goodness of Josiah (whom we shall meet in the next few episodes) could not counteract its effects (see 2 Kings 23:26: 'Still the Lord did not turn from the fierceness of his great wrath, by which his anger was kindled against Judah, because of all the provocations with which Manasseh had provoked him'). Although Manasseh was not blamed for the entirety of Judah's destruction, a large portion of blame was laid at his door.

Part of Manasseh's crime was the overturning of the good reforms of Hezekiah. Many of his predecessors had simply allowed the existing altars and worship places to remain: Manasseh, we are told, specifically reintroduced them, and not only in Israel as a whole but in the temple itself (v. 4). This was one of the greatest crimes of all because the temple was the one place where God had chosen to dwell in the midst of the people. To introduce the images of other gods there was to symbolise a total turning away, which was much worse than Ahaz's attempt to juggle and keep together God's demands with those of his human overlords.

Numerous scholars have suggested that part of what was happening in this chapter was the reintroduction of the practice of seeing Asherah as the consort of God, thus combining Baal worship with Israelite worship. Asherah was a mother goddess in Baal religion and was considered to be the consort of El; there is some evidence, however, that in Judah some people worshipped her as the consort not of El but of the Lord.

This might be indicated by the introduction of an image of Asherah in the temple (v. 7).

It was these actions, the Deuteronomistic historians tell us, that made Judah's destruction inevitable. Up to this point there was always the possibility that the Judeans might be able to avert disaster (as Hezekiah's reign indicated), but now the die has been cast. The significance of what will happen is communicated not so much by the dreadful threat of destruction, but by the simple phrase that the ears of those who hear of Judah's fate will 'tingle'. The Hebrew word has the sense of 'quiver with fear': the events are to be so frightening that the ears of those who hear of them will shiver with fear involuntarily.

2 The finding of the book of the law

2 Kings 22

Manasseh's son, Amon, continued to act in the same way as his father. After his death, however, Josiah came to the throne and he transformed the worship of Judah. In fact, the implication of the text here is that he was even better than David because he acted like David but did not 'turn aside to the right or the left' (v. 2); that is, he did not leave the path that God had set out for him (unlike David, who did turn aside on more than one occasion). The first manifestation of Josiah's righteousness was his desire to restore and rebuild the temple, so he sent his servants into the temple storehouses to find out how much money was there that could be used in the reform. While there, the servants found 'the book of the law' in the storehouses—presumably lost somewhere in a dusty corner (v. 8).

Scholars have seen great significance in the finding of the book of the law. Most are agreed that it contained, if not the book of Deuteronomy itself (which, many scholars think, reached a final form later than the reign of Josiah), at least some of the ancient laws that were eventually written down in Deuteronomy. It was a symbol of how lost the nation of Judah had become, that the collection of laws which gave the people guidance on how to follow God properly had been allowed to sit in a corner gathering dust, unnoticed and unread. It should be noted, however, that there is little agreement among scholars about how old this particular collection of laws was: some think it was an ancient collection of the earliest laws of Israel, while others think that it was written even during the reign of Josiah and deposited shortly before it was found.

The impact of the book of the law, however, is of more importance than its history, because by reading it Josiah and his followers were able, at least temporarily, to reintroduce to Judah the true worship of God. Josiah's response to the finding of the book was immediate and heartfelt: he tore his clothes as a symbol of his own and the whole nation's sorrow at what they had done, since he clearly recognised that the people's actions were far from what God required of them.

In order to find out the significance of the book, Josiah consulted a prophet associated with the royal court (Huldah was married to the keeper of the wardrobe). No comment is made in the text about the fact that Huldah was a rare *female* prophet (others include Miriam, Deborah, the wife of Isaiah and Noadiah) but her message was as one might expect—that judgment was now inevitable. The one glimmer of hope she could offer was that it would be postponed because of Josiah's righteousness.

3 Josiah's reforms

2 Kings 23:1–24

It is a sign of his character that Josiah engaged in reform simply because it was the right thing to do, and despite the fact that it could not, ultimately, alter the fate of his nation. His first action was to gather the whole nation together and make a covenant before God. This covenant called to mind and re-enacted the Sinai covenant, which Moses had made on behalf of the people with God. Thus Josiah was signifying that he, like Moses, was making a covenant with God on behalf of the people.

We then see Josiah beginning to clear out all non-Yahwistic worship from the nation—breaking down altars, driving out prophets, priests and temple prostitutes and, in short, preventing any semblance of Canaanite worship from taking place in the land. Two incidents in particular are worthy of note. The first is the prevention of the burning of children at Topheth (v. 10). Topheth was in the valley of Hinnom (in Hebrew *Ge Hinnom*, from which the Greek word *Gehenna* is derived, often translated into English as 'hell') and was the place where the city's rubbish was burnt. The location is associated here with the offering of children to Molech (another name for Baal) as a sacrifice—a tradition also mentioned in Leviticus 18:21 and 20:2–4. It is unknown, however, whether the practice ever actually existed, since there are no records of it outside the Bible and it may have been meant to symbolise abhorrence for the worship of Baal.

The other feature of note is the reference (in vv. 17–18) to the bones of the man of God who had prophesied the destruction of the altar at Bethel (see 1 Kings 13). The Deuteronomistic historians draw our attention, yet again, to the fact that this prophecy has been fulfilled exactly as was promised by the man of God. One more time, therefore, God's word as spoken through the prophets is demonstrated to have come true, even though it is a hundred or so years since the prophecy was made.

The culmination of Josiah's reform was the celebration of the Passover. Some people have taken verse 22 to mean that the Passover had not been celebrated at all from the period of the Judges to the reign of Josiah. This is evidently not the case, as 2 Chronicles 30:1 refers to Hezekiah's celebration of the Passover. Rather, the uniqueness of Josiah's Passover lay in the fact that he celebrated it according to the book of the law but also in Jerusalem. It was therefore a family-centred festival (as Exodus 12:1—13:16 requires) but was located in the city where God had chosen to dwell.

4 The death of Josiah

2 Kings 23:29–37

After his glorious reign, the death of Josiah comes as something of a disappointment, although it is in character with the rest of Josiah's reforms. In 612BC the Assyrians suffered a defeat at the hands of their rivals to the south, Babylon. It was this weakening and subsequent defeat of the Assyrian empire that gave Josiah the freedom to make his reforms: unlike Hezekiah, he did not have to fear the retribution of the Assyrian empire when he threw off their influence. In 609BC (the year in which the events described in this passage took place) Pharaoh Neco sought to fight with Babylon over the Assyrian empire, and to gain influence over the lands that had been theirs. So he went north to join with the remnants of the Assyrian army and fight against the Babylonians.

This is the context of the battle described in today's passage, since Josiah rode out with his army to fight against the Egyptians, presumably in an attempt to prevent them from joining with the Assyrians against the Babylonians. This attempt ended in disaster and the death of Josiah. The battle between the Egyptians and Assyrians went ahead but the outcome was inconclusive. As a result of Josiah's death, Judah fell under the control of the Egyptians until they, in their turn, were defeated by the Babylonians four years later, when control of the land then passed on, again, to the Babylonians.

The question that puzzles scholars is why Josiah sought to intervene in the battle between such great empires. The most obvious explanation is that it fits in with his reforms. Josiah saw Assyria as the empire that had imposed ungodly ways upon Judah, and attempted to ensure that, after their period of weakness, they were unable to reinforce their power over the land. The sad and slightly ironic outcome of his intervention, however, was that he ensured a swift takeover of Judah first by the Egyptians and then by the Babylonians. The very event he was trying to avoid was achieved by his ill-timed actions.

Thus the great and glorious king, viewed by many as the new David come to save his people, died a sad and inglorious death attempting to affect the global politics of the world around him. He seems to have confused his own role in Judah with the wider political scene. Josiah was called to redeem and reform his own land, but at the end he seemed to be trying to affect the fate of politics far beyond that land—and, in doing so, achieved only his own death.

5 The Babylonians conquer Judah

2 Kings 24

Like the death of Josiah in the previous episode, the events described in this chapter make sense only when understood against the background of the historical events of the day.

The effect of Josiah's death, as we noted above, was to bring Judah under the control of Egypt for about four years, until Egypt in its turn was conquered by the rapidly growing Babylonian empire and Judah was passed on to Babylonian control. When the Egyptians took control of Judah, they deposed Josiah's elder son, Jehoahaz, who had reigned for only three months, and replaced him with Eliakim, renamed Jehoiakim, Josiah's second son. The reason for this is presumably that Jehoahaz continued to follow his father's anti-Egyptian policy, whereas Jehoiakim was more friendly towards Egypt. This position seemed to cause him to oppose the Babylonians (who continued to be enemies of Egypt) and to rebel against their power (v. 1).

As a result of this action, Nebuchadrezzar (sometimes called Nebuchadnezzar in the Bible) sent raiding parties of mercenaries into Judah (v. 2) to unsettle the nation until Babylon could muster an army to fight against it. It is not clear precisely how long it was between the rebellion and the arrival of the Babylonian army, but the rebellion probably took place some time between 600 and 599BC. Before the Babylonians arrived, however, Jehoiakim died, leaving his son, confusingly named Jehoiakin, to face the army. Jehoiakin surrendered swiftly to the Babylonians, which probably explains why the royal court, at least, was treated leniently and taken off into exile in the Babylonian court.

This policy of removing the ruling élite and relocating them in Babylon was a common means of subjugating the lands within the Babylonian empire. Logic dictated that nations were much less likely to rebel if their rulers and the religious and economic élite of the land were taken away.

By this stage in the story, there is little time or necessity to explain why the exile was taking place. The books of Joshua, Judges, 1 and 2 Samuel and 1 and 2 Kings all lay out the history of how the nation had reached this point. In the eyes of the Deuteronomistic historians, the events described in chapter 24 are not due to the actions of Josiah, or even of Jehoiakim, but to the lengthy deterioration of the people of God and their inability to learn their lesson from what had happened to their brothers and sisters in the northern kingdom about 100 years before. This is all summed up in the short half verse in 24:20: 'Indeed, Jerusalem and Judah so angered the Lord that he expelled them from his presence.' Judah has been cast out of God's presence: how far they have fallen from being the specially chosen people of God whom God loved so much.

6 Exile and hope?

Chapter 25 finishes the story, with a slight glimmer of hope at the end. Jehoiakin was replaced on the throne by another of Josiah's sons, Zedekiah (Jehoiakin's uncle, 24:17), whose role was to care for the land on behalf of the Babylonians. However, he continued the policy of opposition to Babylon begun by his brother Jehoiakim before his death, and so rebelled against the Babylonians. This caused the Babylonians to return to Jerusalem in around 589BC and besiege the city for around two years. After a severe famine within the city, the army breached the walls and pursued the king and his followers. When they caught Zedekiah, they were much less lenient than they had been to Jehoiakin, slaughtering his sons before his eyes and then blinding him. This was seen as a just punishment for his breach of promise to the Babylonians.

After this, the Babylonians took all but the poorest of the people into exile and appointed Gedeliah to rule over the land (v. 22)—the first non-Davidic ruler in Judah since the time of King David. Evidently this was too much for the remnants of David's household and someone called Ishmael—of David's family but not necessarily close to the succession of the throne—assassinated Gedeliah (v. 25). At this point, Judah was at the lowest possible ebb—without a king or any of the ruling or religious élite, with a city and land in ruins, and little hope of any brighter future.

The very end of the story, however, contains the slightest glimmer of hope. Perhaps, just perhaps, all is not lost. The true king lived in Babylon, dined at the royal court and was cared for by the Babylonians. Beyond utter hopelessness and despair, life went on. The question now was what that life might look like in the future.

Guidelines

Although it is hard to see, the Deuteronomistic historians do leave us at the end of 2 Kings with the merest whiff of hope. The logical end of the story would have been the assassination of Gedeliah, the moment when all hope for the land of Judah after the exile was extinguished, but 2 Kings does not end there. Instead it ends, rather strangely to us, with an account of how the king survived and in fact thrived in exile. It is this ending that alerts us to the fact that 2 Kings is, in an odd way, a book filled with hope. The purpose of the story is not simply to tell the exiles that their hardships were their own fault but to remind them that their fate was not random, hopeless misfortune but the direct result of their actions. By extension, then, different actions in the future would produce different results.

Even at the time when the deepest despair seems inevitable, God gives the hint of hope. All may be lost right now, but in the future there is potential for redemption and renewal. The powerful lesson of 2 Kings is that this redemption and renewal can come only through a thorough and thoughtful learning of all that history can teach. The future of Judah is bound up in its history—if only the people of God can comprehend what this might mean.

2 Kings contains what are, for many people, a number of unpleasant and unpalatable stories marked by God's anger and retribution. If we can begin to see beyond this, however, we can encounter a message that our world needs to hear as much today as it did then. Actions have consequences and those who wish to live well in the world, in the way that God requires, need to learn discernment—a discernment that comprehends the past so that it can transform the future. Without this gift, our world too may find itself heading towards disaster.

FURTHER READING

This further reading list is largely the same as for 1 Kings, with an additional recommendation for a book on Asherah and her role in the ancient world. As for 1 Kings, it is useful to have and to use a good Bible atlas such as A. Curtis, *Oxford Bible Atlas* (OUP, 2007) or P. Lawrence, *The Lion Atlas of Bible History* (Lion, 2006).

S. Dawes, *1 and 2 Kings* (People's Bible Commentary), BRF, 2001.

I. Provan, V.P. Long and T. Longman, *A Biblical History of Israel*, Westminster John Knox, 2003.

J. Drane, *Introducing the Old Testament*, Lion, 2000.

On Asherah see W.G. Dever, *Did God Have a Wife? Archaeology and Folk Religion in Ancient Israel*, Eerdmans, 2005.

THE BIRTH OF JESUS IN LUKE

This year we will look at the familiar Christmas story through Luke's Gospel. It is a rich account, full of expectation and fulfilment, hopes and fears, and of God's action challenging and going beyond what was expected. Luke will be our Gospel in 2010, following on from this study of the first two chapters. We will think more about the date and origin of the Gospel then. For now, though, we can note that there are connections between ourselves this Christmas and the purpose of Luke. As we will see in our first reading, Luke was written for those who already knew the story of Jesus, but aimed at revealing more clearly the truth of those events—including the inner truth of how, through them, God was fulfilling his purposes. As we live through Christmas these next weeks, with its multiple overlapping agendas, pressures and delights, Luke stands alongside us, whispering in our ears, pointing out to us how God's plan was being unfolded in the events then and challenging us to look to see how God's plan might be unfolding in our world today.

Unless otherwise indicated, quotations in these notes have been taken from the New International Version of the Bible.

1 Introduction

Luke 1:1–4

Luke begins his book with an introduction, explaining the purpose of the book to his readers, in particular to Theophilus (v. 3). Both Luke's Gospel and its sequel, the Acts of the Apostles, are dedicated to this unknown figure. Perhaps it was not a person at all, for the name means 'lover of God'. Perhaps the Gospel is addressed to all who seek after God.

Luke admits that others before him have written accounts of Jesus' life, death and resurrection, and probably included are some or all of Mark, Matthew and John. Nevertheless, Luke chose to write as well. The reason why is probably revealed in his stress on 'carefully investigated', an 'orderly account' and 'you may know the certainty' (NRSV). While Luke does not criticise the previous writers, he perhaps feels that the facts about Jesus have not always been made as clear as they should be. Compared to Matthew and Luke, Mark is limited in what it contains (for example, it does not have the Lord's Prayer). Matthew does not present an 'orderly' account: it gathers teaching together into blocks, while Luke presents Jesus' teaching mixed in with incidents 'on the way' in a believable 'order'.

Luke also tells his readers how he has got his information. He himself is not an eyewitness (at least, not one 'from the first') but his material has come from those 'servants of the word' who were eyewitnesses. This concern for eyewitness testimony occurs elsewhere in the New Testament (1 John 1:1; Hebrews 2:3). Theophilus appears to have been taught about Jesus already; perhaps he was already a follower of Jesus. What Luke's Gospel provides is certainty about what has been taught. Stories about Jesus need not be accepted just on hearsay: Luke has gone back to the people who were there, and carefully prepared this orderly account of what actually happened. His approach here, as elsewhere, is in keeping with the standards of contemporaneous history-writing. His Gospel has been crafted to appeal to and gain respect among a broad audience in his day.

As well as accuracy, Luke stresses another theme: 'the things that have been fulfilled'. Jesus' actions were not simply events, but were fulfilments of God's plan, what God had promised. The next two chapters make this point very strongly, but it continues through this book and its sequel.

It is worth considering whether we, like Luke, attempt to present the gospel in a way that will commend it to people in our day. What would that mean? And do we believe in God's plan? If so, where do we feel we fit into it? Finally, does the fact that there are four Gospels concern us? Do we secretly feel that we would prefer it if God had just given us one, or can we see value in their overlapping portraits of Jesus?

2 Zechariah and Elizabeth: announcement

Luke 1:5–17

Luke chooses to begin his story not with Jesus' birth but with that of John and the prophecies that preceded it. Crucially, this is a thoroughly Jewish story. Zechariah and Elizabeth have impeccable credentials: both are drawn from priestly families and pious in a traditional Jewish fashion. This supports a point that Luke makes time and time again: the story of Jesus is not of a rebellious breakaway from Judaism but rather of the fulfilment of God's promises. Indeed, the situation has echoes of three previous great moments in Jewish history. Isaac, through whom all God's promises to Abraham were to be fulfilled (Genesis 18 to 21), Samson, who defeated Israel's enemies (Judges 13—16) and Samuel, who would be the greatest of the judges (1 Samuel 1—3), were all born to women deemed to be barren. The link between John and Samson is made stronger by the ban on 'wine or strong drink' (v. 15, NRSV).

The birth of John (the name means 'gift from God') is to be a blessing to Zechariah and Elizabeth, removing the shame (in their culture) of childlessness, but it is also much more. The end of the angel's announcement echoes the final words of Malachi, the last of the prophets in our Old Testament: 'I will send you the prophet Elijah before the great and terrible day of the Lord comes. He will turn the hearts of parents to their children and the hearts of children to their parents, so that I will not come and strike the land with a curse' (4:5–6, NRSV).

Four points emerge. First, God is doing something new to fulfil his promises of old. Second, John's role is a positive one, bringing many of the people of Israel back to God, restoring broken relationships and revealing the right way to live. Third, John will be a powerful man: Elijah was the greatest miracle worker in Jewish history, alongside Moses, famous for his battle with pagan religions and an oppressive and murderous king (1 Kings 17—21). Fourth, there is a note of expectancy: Malachi's prophet comes before 'the day'; the angel says that John's role is one of preparation. What is really important will come afterwards. But Malachi has a note of threat: 'terrible day… strike the land with a curse'. The angel does not mention this threat: perhaps what God is doing will be better than expected.

Expectations are powerful. They can motivate action even when times are bad, they can support endurance, but they can also produce frustration and bitterness. Elizabeth, Zechariah and the whole people of God had had to wait for many years, but now the fulfilment was to be good beyond expectations. What do we wait for?

3 Zechariah and Elizabeth: response

Luke 1:18–25

Who can blame Zechariah for asking for some proof? After all, it would be a miracle for him and Elizabeth even to have a son, never mind everything else the angel had said. The silence imposed on him has a certain irony to it. It seems to be a punishment for his lack of faith, yet it also functions as exactly the sort of 'miraculous sign' that he sought. This is certainly how it worked: his dumbness proved to the people that he had seen a vision.

The mention of the 'proper time' (v. 20) continues the theme of fulfilment. It has been many centuries since Malachi prophesied. Nevertheless, God has not forgotten his promise; it will be fulfilled at the proper time, which is now approaching. Gabriel also uses the word 'to tell good news' (v. 19), which is a key note in the book. The Gospel of Luke and Acts are books about the telling of the good news (see, in particular, Jesus' definition of his mission in Luke 4:18–19).

The reaction of the people is typical of many of the reactions throughout the book. They realise that something is happening, that God is acting in some way, but they do not truly understand the meaning of the events that they see. They are bemused bystanders, watching what God is doing. Here, there is no blame to be attached to them: they do not understand only because Zechariah is dumb. However, when John and Jesus come speaking the message clearly, still many of them do not understand what God is doing among them (for example, Luke 10:13–15; 11:29–32; 19:41–44).

The idea that God shows favour to those whom the world despises, who are in disgrace, is also important throughout the book. It is the great theme of Mary's song later in this chapter; it is announced as Jesus' mission (4:18–19); many times we will see it fulfilled in Jesus' dealing with people.

How do we react to God's activity? Many of us are cynical, protecting ourselves from disappointment, shy to attribute events to God. Or we see that something is happening but stand on the sidelines, nervous perhaps of what it might mean to be involved with God's promises. As the angel said, though, what God is doing is 'good news'. More personally, do you bear a shame that you wish God would take away?

4 Mary: announcement

We can see the enormity of what is being said to Mary by comparing this announcement with the one to Zechariah. For Elizabeth, a child will remove her disgrace; for Mary, however, pregnancy—God's purpose—will bring scandal and disgrace. For Elizabeth, the child will be a miracle but will still be born of her and her husband. Indeed, the announcement of the pregnancy comes to Zechariah, and he will name the child. In contrast, Mary is alone. The announcement comes direct to her, independent of her betrothed husband, who presumably, like everyone else, will assume she has committed adultery. She, not Joseph, is to name the child. Here the miracle is of a different order—conception involving only Mary and God.

John ('gift of God') has a role in preparing the people. Mary's child, however, is to be called Jesus, which means 'God is salvation'. One will prepare while the other will complete. The angel's words to Mary (vv. 32–33) pick up the prophecy given to the great King David himself: 'When your days are over… I will raise up your offspring to succeed you… and I will establish the throne of his kingdom for ever. I will be his father, and he will be my son' (2 Samuel 7:12–14). Joseph was a descendant of David; Jesus will be called God's son; he will have the throne of his father David; he will reign over Israel as David did; his kingdom will never end.

The angel gives a direct answer to Mary's question 'How can this be?', explaining that the divine Spirit itself will produce the life within Mary's womb (vv. 35–37). There is no sense here of the anthropomorphisms of Greek myths in which gods take human form and have sex with women. The angel also answers the implied question, 'Do such miracles happen?' Elizabeth provides the example: if God can produce life in the womb of an old woman who has always been barren, he can surely do it within Mary.

Mary's final words are the epitome of obedience and acceptance. God's plan is great for others but it will be costly for her. The challenge to us is obvious. Many of us secretly wish that God would use us in some great way in his purposes; maybe we feel that, with God's support, we could really make a difference in our church or community. But Mary reminds us that being open to God's purposes might involve a cost. Would we be as willing to pay that price as Mary was?

5 Mary: response

Both Mary and Elizabeth are caught up in the same divine plan. More could be said about their meeting, but today we focus on Mary's song—frequently called the Magnificat—a mainstay of choral church music. The song falls into three sections. First, Mary praises God for what he has done personally for her (vv. 46–49a). She is nobody special and yet, as Elizabeth has just said, now she will be called blessed. However, the 'great things' that Mary praises God for doing—causing her to become pregnant outside marriage—would seem objectively to be a great calamity. Even if it serves a divine purpose, it will be a hard road to walk. Mary's song exhibits no such sentiments, though, such is her delight to be part of God's purposes.

The second section (vv. 49b–53) focuses on God's attributes and actions. He is holy, powerful, righteous and distinct from the ways of the world. However, he is not aloof and uncaring. On the contrary, alongside his holiness is unending mercy for 'those who fear him' (v. 50)—those who revere him, who respond to him as Mary has done. Notice also the three statements focusing on the theme of reversal. God is mighty and destroys those who are proud (that is, the opposite of Mary). He brings down rulers and exalts the humble (like Mary). He acts to help the poor and opposes the rich. On Mary's lips these are not just general descriptions of what God is like; they also correspond to the events in which she is caught up. The stress on reversal—rulers/humble, rich/hungry—reflects Mary's humble opinion of herself. By choosing to act through her, not through the wealthy or powerful, God has demonstrated his favour for the humble and lowly.

The third part of the song (vv. 54–55) turns from Mary in particular to Israel in general. The events taking place do not bring blessing on Mary alone. On the contrary, God's plan is for the birth of a boy who is to have the throne of David and rule for ever. Israel will be restored from its current place as an occupied region of the Roman Empire. The whole of Israel is in subjugation under the Romans. Thus, Mary's status is doubly low—she is an unmarried mother-to-be, of a defeated and subjugated people—which only serves to highlight God's mercy and the reversal of status that he brings. Furthermore, in doing this God is fulfilling his promises of old.

God's purposes involve reversal, a 'bias towards the poor', but where does this leave us? In our daily life, in this country, in the world, are we among the rulers or the humble, the hungry or the rich? Are we proud or, like Mary, do we rejoice to be part of God's purposes, despite the cost?

6 The birth of John

Luke 1:57–66

Joy and mercy, the dominant themes of this chapter, emerge once more. The Lord has been merciful to Elizabeth; indeed, the words of Mary's song about 'lifting up the humble' apply to Elizabeth as well. Notice also that the joy is not just a private one: the whole community shares it.

The incident of the boy's naming brings to completion the angel's message to Zechariah. However, there is more in the naming than simply obedience to the angel. Great stress is put on how surprising it is that he should be named John. This is a departure from the norm: the boy's name is 'to everyone's astonishment' (v. 63). The miracle of Zechariah's temporary dumbness serves only to heighten the sense of amazement. This child is going to be special; he is going to defy expectations, for the Lord is with him. This is recognised by the neighbours, who are filled with awe—the typical reaction to God's actions. God has arranged his birth for a particular purpose. That purpose had been told to Zechariah in the temple, and in the following verses Zechariah will declare it publicly.

This takes us back to the issue of expectations—our own and those of the community in which we live and work. The people shared Elizabeth's joy, welcoming her expectation-defying babe. What is there not to celebrate about the birth of a child? But there are limits. When the mother starts trying to say what the child's name should be, the people are less welcoming: it was not the mother's place to decide such things. To make it worse, the name was not conventional. Societies, and churches, have a very strong built-in mechanism that allows a little bit of change, a little bit of challenging expectations, but no more. The young people being 'showcased' each Sunday before they leave to their groups is fine; the suggestion that occasionally the young people should stay in church and the adults go out to groups is not. Helping with a soup run for the homeless is OK; demanding that houses should be provided for them is not. This is not surprising, for too much change brings the possibility of the sort of reversal that Mary spoke of—filling the hungry and sending the rich away. We, like them, can easily ask for God to act and rejoice when he does, but also start to wonder nervously when God does not seem to be following our script.

Guidelines

Three themes emerge from this week's readings: expectations, obedience and reversal. We have seen the people's expectation that God would act—their hopes for a better world—as well as their expectation that nothing should change too much. Mary's obedience to God's plan, despite the personal cost, gives good reason for all generations to call her blessed. Her song begins the great theme of reversal—the hungry being filled, the rich being sent away empty—which will reverberate throughout the Gospel.

As we approach Christmas, it is worth meditating on these themes. What expectations do we have this Christmas? That nothing will change too much, or that God will act? Looking into the coming year, what are we waiting for? What are we looking to God to fulfil? Are we too jaded or accepting of the way the world is to dare to expect change from God?

'Yet what I can I give him: give my heart' says the Christmas carol by Christina Rossetti. Mary opened her heart to God and accepted her calling, despite the cost. What of us? Is God asking us to say 'yes' to something this Christmas time?

Perhaps most disturbingly of all, we need to ask, are we among the rich who will be sent away, or the hungry who will be fed? Put another way, are we willing to be part of God's reversal, or do we resist it?

1 Zechariah's prophecy

Luke 1:67–80

Zechariah's prophecy, well known in traditional churches as the Benedictus, builds on and amplifies the angel's announcement of John's birth, the announcement to Mary and Mary's song. This prophecy answers the neighbours' question, 'What then will this child become?' (v. 66, NRSV) in a revealing way, for the first part of Zechariah's song is not about John but about what God is doing through the yet unborn Jesus. Jesus is the salvation from the house of David, the fulfilment of God's promise to Abraham (vv. 69, 73). Then, at verse 76, Zechariah turns to talk about John himself, building on the angelic message (see 1:13–17). The end of the prophecy echoes Isaiah 9:2–7, which, with its talk of establishing David's throne for ever, seems to be talking again of Jesus' work. There is a point in this apparent confusion. John and his role cannot be understood apart from Jesus'. Even though Jesus has not yet been born, Zechariah can talk about him in the past tense because of his confidence that what God has started in the birth of John, he will surely finish with Jesus.

The wording in verse 76 is particularly striking, for John, as the 'prophet of the Most High', is said to go 'before the Lord to prepare the way for him'. This phrase echoes Isaiah 40:3, which will be quoted directly about John in Luke 3:4–6. The logic of both chapters 1 and 3, the inter-weaving of the story of John and Jesus and the words said to Mary (where Jesus is said to be the 'son of the Most High', 1:32, 35), all suggest that John is preparing the way for Jesus. John is a prophet. Jesus is more than that: he is 'the Lord', a term which, in the context of Isaiah 40, clearly points to God himself. All these ancient prophecies are about to be fulfilled. There is a period of waiting, however, for John needs to grow to maturity first. Nevertheless, the divine plan has been launched.

John was to have a highly exalted role (see 7:28), but even he is just a part of the divine plan. He has a role to play but it is not about him. Some of us long to have a part in God's plans: maybe this Christmas we are being called, like John was, to prepare the way for God and bring knowledge of salvation (not of judgment or condemnation, but the true Christmas good news of salvation). Others can easily see ways in which we can contribute but find it hard to accept that we are not centre stage.

2 The birth of Jesus

Luke 2:1–7

After all the excitement of the previous chapter, the story now has a more prosaic tone. In the terms of Luke's introduction (1:1–4), the end of the last chapter perhaps focused more on 'the things that have been fulfilled among us', while this section has a tone more suited to 'an orderly account'. The facts and figures are recounted (and note that this is done without any assumption that the reader is acquainted with Jewish life: the date is expressed by reference to the Roman emperor, and the fact is mentioned that Bethlehem is the town of David).

The story is told almost as if the previous chapter had not been there. We are told again that Joseph is from the house of David, and that Mary is his pregnant fiancée. No word is mentioned of the angelic message to Mary or the true origin of the child. It is as if this paragraph represents an outsiders', or 'objective', view of what is happening, while the pre-vious chapter has revealed the true meaning of the events.

There are two further points of note. First (v. 4), David is mentioned twice in one sentence. Although nothing more explicit is made of it here, it is a reminder of the prophecies in the previous chapter. Second, we are reminded of the lowly state of the Jewish people at the time, and of Mary herself. They are not free: despite Mary's pregnancy, Joseph has no choice but to travel to register because the Roman emperor wants him to. They need rescuing from their enemies. Mary herself has to lay her firstborn son in a manger—an animal food trough—because they cannot get anywhere better to stay. She is one of the humble who need lifting up.

The simplicity of this account of the birth of Jesus, compared to all that came before and soon follows, is significant. It reminds us that the great events of history, the great acts of God, are not necessarily dramatic or miraculous. A woman from an occupied corner of the Roman Empire has a child and shelters him in an animal trough. Who would notice this non-event? Yet it stands at the centre of history. We need to pray that God would give us 'eyes of faith' to see the true meaning of seemingly insignificant events around us, and the humility to pursue what is right, not what is dramatic or newsworthy.

3 Announced to the shepherds

Luke 2:8–20

The theme of the exaltation of the lowly continues with the announcement to the shepherds. Shepherds were at the bottom of society. They were landless, with no trade or tools, and no means of supporting themselves other than hiring themselves out to the wealthy to watch their flocks. Yet it was to them that the angelic message came: indeed, Mary's song suggests that it was people like this who were at the centre of God's plan. The appearance of this angel has similarities with the appearances to Zechariah and Mary: the humans react with fear but the angel says, 'Do not be afraid' (v. 10). However, there are differences. This seems a far more public and open announcement. The glory of the Lord is shining all around and the heavenly host (army) appears. His birth is 'good news of great joy for all the people' (even shepherds!) (v. 10, NRSV), not a private matter.

For the first time, the word 'Christ' (the Greek translation of the Hebrew 'Messiah' or 'anointed one') is applied to Jesus (v. 11). Here it is combined with a reference to David, picking up the idea of a descendant of David ruling his kingdom for ever. Various Old Testament passages link the 'son of David' to 'the anointed one', such as Psalm 2, and Isaiah 11:1–9. Others in Jesus' day were also linking these passages together (for example, those who wrote the Dead Sea Scrolls), although there was no clear sense of what 'the Messiah' would be. Some of the Dead Sea Scrolls talk of two Messiahs—a priestly and a kingly one. The effect here in Luke is to weave together various threads of prophecy: now is the time for all the divine promises to be fulfilled.

The shepherds' response is straightforward. They go 'with haste' (v. 16, NRSV) and find the baby. They have been readily given a sign (v. 12: compare Zechariah and Mary, who had to ask for one) because God's plan has already started to be fulfilled. There seems a huge contrast between a baby in a feeding-trough and 'a saviour… Christ the Lord' (v. 11). Nevertheless, they believe what they have been told, and spread the word (vv. 17–18).

Meanwhile, Mary 'ponders in her heart' what is happening, what has been announced publicly about the baby she has just borne. After the long months of pregnancy and the shame arising from it, it must have been a comfort to hear a confirmation of what the angel had told her before it had all begun. Between them, Mary and the shepherds give us two responses to God's actions: the extravert, responding quickly and sharing the news with others, and the introvert, treasuring and pondering in their heart. Our personality leads most of us in one or other of these directions; perhaps we would benefit from trying out the other.

4 A light to the Gentiles

Luke 2:21–35

We begin with a reminder that Jesus' story is a thoroughly Jewish one. Just as Zechariah and Elizabeth were portrayed earlier as pious Jews (1:5–6), so too Jesus' parents follow the Jewish law and tradition (vv. 21–24). Jesus is to be a saviour of the people, not someone leading a rebellion against their customs.

Simeon recognises Jesus (despite the fact that he is merely a tiny baby) as being the 'consolation of Israel' (v. 25) for which he has been waiting. The phrase is equivalent to 'salvation' (v. 30), but evokes the sense of the nation as a downtrodden, suffering people. He is happy to die because he knows that the long period of Israel's subjugation is coming to an end. He has seen in advance what will in time be public ('in the sight of all people', v. 31).

Then Simeon says something startling: Jesus is 'a light for revelation to the Gentiles' (v. 32; see Isaiah 49:6). So far in Luke, God's plan has only ever seemed to be rescue for the Jewish people—even, by implication, putting down their Gentile (non-Jewish) enemies. Simeon, however, the pious Jew (v. 25) in the centre of the Jewish temple, proclaims that Jesus is going to do more than just rescue Israel; he will even bring light to the Gentiles (for they too are 'living in darkness' as Zechariah said, 1:79). No wonder Joseph and Mary marvelled.

Simeon's final words to Mary, though, cast a shadow over all this. Jesus will not simply bring salvation to Israel: he will cause the fall as well as the rising of many, and will be spoken against. Simeon's words have broken the idea of Jewish exclusivism. Jesus will cause the falling of many within Israel, while bringing light to (some) Gentiles. The focus seems to be 'the thoughts of many hearts' (v. 35). Jesus will reveal people's hearts, whether they be Jewish or not. Perhaps Mary's song that God 'has filled the hungry with good things but has sent the rich away empty' has a more universal scope. The division that Jesus brings within Israel is a theme that continues throughout the Gospel of Luke but is picked up even more strongly in Acts. It is easy for those of us who are Gentiles to read this and rejoice that God's mercy flowed even to us. However, we should also hear the challenge to any exclusive attitudes that we have: Jesus brings light to the 'outsiders' and some 'insiders' will fall: 'some are last who will be first, and some are first who will be last' (13:30, NRSV).

The final words, 'a sword will piece your own soul too' (v. 35), continue the undercurrent that these great acts of God will also bring pain for some, challenging the all-too-common belief that if we obey God we will be saved from suffering.

5 Anna

Luke 2:36–40

Anna is similar to Simeon in that both represent Jewish piety, although she is explicitly said to be a prophet. It is a notable feature of Luke that an incident focused on a man is often paired with one focused on a woman. For example, in the previous chapter, an angel appears to Zechariah and to Mary and each of them speaks a hymn of praise. Later Jesus will heal a man and a woman in similar circumstances on a sabbath (6:6–11; 13:10–17), and he will tell of both a man and a woman searching for the lost (15:3–7, 8–10).

Thus Simeon and Anna should probably be taken together as a 'gender pair'. Simeon's words are recorded, while Anna's are not; Simeon speaks only to Joseph and Mary, Anna broadcasts the message to everyone who, like Simeon, is 'looking for the redemption of Jerusalem' (v. 38, NRSV). Nevertheless, it is intriguing to note that it is the 'lowly'— first the shepherds and now Anna—who are said to spread the message. In the same way, the first messengers of the resurrection are the (lower status) women, not the (higher status) apostles (24:5–10). This is a natural response to the fulfilment of expectation: Anna has been waiting earnestly (v. 37) and now, perhaps overhearing Simeon's words, she feels that fulfilment has come. Even so, we note again that fulfilment hadn't actually come yet: seeing the beginning of God's plan was enough for her to have confidence that the redemption of Jerusalem would now take place.

The final verse seems just to be rounding off the birth narrative.

However, it reminds us of God's patience. We might like everything to happen now, if not yesterday, but God was prepared for this plan to unfold slowly, at a human pace. As so often in the Bible, we see organic words like 'growth' used for the divine plan, not mechanical or managerial words of 'actions' or 'solutions'. If the kingdom of heaven is like a seed growing slowly, so too is the formation of holy character in us, as it was even in Jesus. Are we conscious of that growth? Are there virtues that we are cultivating, and vices we are striving to separate from?

6 The boy Jesus

Luke 2:41–52

Ancient writers did not have the same understanding of human psychology and development as we do. When biographers such as Plutarch (a near contemporary of Luke, who wrote 'lives' of famous Greeks and Romans) recorded incidents taken from childhood, those incidents revealed how the child had the characteristics for which the adult later became famous (just as, today, a parent whose adult child has become an engineer will tell stories of how, when the child was two, he or she was always building things from Lego).

Therefore, we should not look to this story for insight into Jesus' development, but rather see it as a lens through which to look at his adult life. There are two main points. First, we see Jesus travelling as a pilgrim to Jerusalem, then sitting teaching in the temple courts, in his 'Father's house' (v. 49). He travels to Jerusalem later in the Gospel (9:51; 19:37–41) and teaches in the temple, but the response he gets is very different ('The chief priests, the scribes, and the leaders of the people kept looking for a way to kill him': 19:47, NRSV). So here we get a glimpse not of the future but of an alternative future—the future that should have been. This shows us the future if Jerusalem had recognised the time of its visitation from God (see 19:44, NRSV), if Jesus had been just for the rising and not for the falling of many in Israel (see 2:34). The effect of this is to highlight that Jesus was not, by nature, opposed to the temple. As we have seen throughout these two chapters, his origins were firmly within traditional, pious Judaism. If the end result was a clash, it was because of how others responded to him.

Second, we enter into Mary and Joseph's anxiety for their lost son—but they are not the only ones to lose Jesus, their son, in the Gospel story. Through this incident we are reminded of the anxiety and distress that God entered into by sending and losing his Son, Jesus. Mary has earlier been told, 'A sword will pierce your own soul too' (2:35); that is true also of God. The wonderful plan of salvation that has been announced by angels and prophets brings great pain to God.

Thus the two chapters of the Christmas story in Luke end on an uncertain note. Jesus is growing in wisdom and stature, in favour with God and humans (v. 52), and we have seen the possibility that he will travel to Jerusalem and be welcomed by the teachers there. But we are also faced with the anxiety and pain of losing a child, even the 'Son of God' (1:35).

Guidelines

We will all have seen nativity scenes this Christmas time. They are so familiar that it is easy to forget how strange they are. They depict something so ordinary, or at least what was ordinary in Jesus' day—a young family, farm animals, poverty. It's a scene you could see down every street, and yet here we are making models and giving them pride of place in our homes and churches. Of course, however, the nativity scene also has angels and 'wise men' bringing fabulous gifts, which point to the fact that this ordinary scene was truly extraordinary.

It takes the eyes of faith, a mind attuned to God's purposes, to see how seemingly ordinary or insignificant events are significant in God's plan. As the carol 'O little town of Bethlehem' has it, 'How silently, how silently the wondrous gift is given'—given while we remain in a 'deep and dreamless sleep'. Furthermore, we need to be prepared for the fact that we will not be centrestage in that plan, that it may well involve patience, waiting and even pain, and that it may disturb our sense of God too. As we leave Christmas behind and start to look to the New Year, we can pray that we would have the eyes to see 'God in the ordinary', and the willingness and courage to accept his purposes.

Joel

The opening description of Joel provides us with little by which to place this short prophetic book, either geographically, historically or with respect to Israel's theological traditions. Much can be deduced, however, from the content (see the first reading for more details). The internal evidence suggests that the prophet's message is meant for Jerusalem and Judah, because of the references to them and the Zion motifs. The lack of reference to northern towns and shrines confirms this idea. In contrast to, for example, Ezekiel, there is nothing to suggest that Joel was in exile. The reference to 'the Greeks' (3:6) has led some to date the prophecy rather late, but by no means all commentators accept this as the proper deduction.

The spiritual context is more pertinent, mainly because this is what the book is dealing with but also because it provides access for us. The main message is that God is activating the curses that were an inherent part of his covenant relationship with 'Israel' because the leaders and the priests have failed God. Whether there are two distinct aspects to the punishment (the devastation of plagues of locusts and invasion by brutal armies) or whether the former is a metaphor for the latter is again disputed.

Beyond this, however, the book can be seen as Judah's confession of her sins. The main purpose is not to condemn but to facilitate repent-ance, including fasting, so that God can act in mercy towards Judah. The devastations are being explained rather than predicted as part of this process. Equally, the judgment on the nations (see ch. 3) is to be understood as the converse of God's restoration of Judah rather than direct vindictiveness against the nations.

1 I am Joel

Joel 1

How do you start a symphony? Should it begin quietly and allure the listeners, enfolding them with nymph-like sounds, or should it commence with a crescendo demanding attention, shocking the audience into engagement? Should it introduce the major theme in the first few notes or keep it hidden, almost deceiving the listeners by giving them a false start? These are some of the issues and some of the opportunities.

So how should you start a prophetic collection? It would be interesting to compare them all, but we can make only a couple of comparisons, with Amos (1:1) and Ezekiel (1:1–3). Here is Joel's opening: 'I am Joel the son of Pethuel. And this is the message the Lord gave to me' (v. 1).

Both Amos and Ezekiel, in different ways, relate their message to historical events—earthquakes, reigning monarchs, and exile—but Joel does not. Joel mentions his lineage but this tells us nothing significant about him—unlike Ezekiel, where the information that he comes from a priestly family gives insight into his message. Ezekiel says that he lives in Babylonia, which will profoundly shape his prophecy. Amos tells us that he is from Tekoa—neither Jerusalem nor Samaria! From Joel's opening lines, we have no idea where he comes from or where he ministers. Finally, we can note that, like Amos, Joel has a 'message', whereas for Ezekiel it is 'visions' that dominate. Are there, then, two different kinds of 'prophecy'? Joel uses the singular 'message', whereas Ezekiel and Amos speak in the plural. Does this indicate that Joel's was a 'one off' prophecy rather than an ongoing ministry?

Even to begin to answer such questions we would need to explore the whole collection of oracles of each prophet. Such collections are themselves as complex and rich as any symphony. Like a musical work, they may incorporate borrowed themes, which could either be incorporated, to stir memories and create moods, or be changed, subtly or deliberately, when they are being used ironically. One thing we need to note about Joel is that many of his motifs are gathered from the covenant curses (and blessings) (see Leviticus 26; Deuteronomy 27—28) and that this provides the 'worldview framework' for his message.

2 The darkest hour

Joel 2:1–11

Blitzkrieg would be an appropriate title for this passage. Living in Coventry, I am well aware of the potent memories of violent destruction caused by war—the terrible bombing, the destruction of buildings, the disorientation and death. But Coventry was not invaded! The enemy troops did not swarm over the ruins and confront the frightened people with brutality and bayonets. Joel's description here of the troops swarming through the land like locusts, and fire consuming everything like a forest blaze, is even more intense. The noise of charging horses, the deadly swish of the sword and the grinding of the chariot wheels are like music from hell. Nothing can stop them: 'They swarm over city walls and enter our homes… just like thieves' (v. 9).

But these images are only half the story. What is it all about? The ultimate terror is that this is the judgment of God: 'Sound the trumpet on Zion, the Lord's sacred hill. Warn everyone to tremble! The judgment day of the Lord is coming soon' (v. 1).

Here we are, right in the middle of Zion theology, the belief that God would protect his temple and his city, come what may. This was an ancient religious confidence, reinforced by the historical experience (during Isaiah's ministry) of the unexpected withdrawal of the Assyrian troops when they appeared to be about to capture Jerusalem (2 Kings 18—19). But it is melded with 'Day of Yahweh' theology, another ancient strand of Israel's faith that God would miraculously intervene and judge those who were attacking or thwarting Israel. By 'judge' was meant 'restore things to the way they should be', to put things to rights, which implied Israel's prosperity and peace and, as necessary, the enemies' discomfort. But now these two themes, which were normally harmonised, are juxtaposed. The Day of Yahweh is playing against Zion theology in a clashing key! Israel's broken covenant means that the intervention of God is against them and not for them. This is required in order to put everything right—including the disobedience of Israel. The call to sound the warning trumpet, issued first to the prophet but relayed by him to the nation, is strident indeed.

As Amos said (see 5:18—20), Yahweh's day of expected deliverance and delight can only be darkness and destruction. God, like a tamed lion, has turned on his people. Each aspect of this passage, understood in the context of the hearers, etches in acid their desperate helplessness, while exposing the fact that they are trapped in their own disobedience. In the New Testament, only Romans 1:18—32 matches the gloom.

3 The trumpet sounds

Joel 2:12–24

When a pistol shot is fired, either someone falls mortally wounded or the athletes power forward for a 100-metre sprint. The same sound can conjure up two antithetical images, one of violent death, the other of energised life. 'Sound the trumpet on Zion' had been heard as the sound of death, the warning of unavoidable and total destruction at the hand of God. Now, in verse 15, it is the sound of life, hope and help.

When a prophet uttered his words from God, they were performative words and not simply rhetorical: they initiated the events about which they spoke. That is why the prophet was so feared. Rather like the situation in which someone is handed a summons by a solicitor, receiving the words made all the difference. But here in the first part of this chapter, Joel's words are painting a scenario rather than fixing the future. 'It isn't too late' (v. 12).

What makes these words even sweeter is that this is not Joel's comment on the situation, as though he can't quite bring himself to fix the nation's fate. They are God's direct words: 'It isn't too late. You can still return to *me* with all your heart' (v. 12, my emphasis: the Hebrew is making the same point but in a different way). The 'me', of course, is not the prophet but God. This is God's personal appeal to his people.

How far the direct quotation from God goes is difficult to determine but it doesn't really matter. The unexpected opportunity depends on two things. It relies on the true nature of God (vv. 13–14; see Exodus 34:6–7), who is merciful, kind and compassionate, and not (like other gods and rulers) keen to get his own back in order to sustain his own reputation. But equally it requires extensive and intensive repentance on the part of the people. The extent is indicated by the involvement of babies and newly-weds, and the intensiveness by the ritual aspects such as fasting and crying, but also by the heart requirements ('all your heart', v. 12; 'broken hearts', v. 13). Indeed, Nehemiah's response to the news of the devastation of Jerusalem fits this description remarkably well (see Nehemiah 1:4).

Finally the priests are told how to intercede, and this is followed by the description of the return of prosperity. So the 'stick' of verses 1–11 is followed by the 'carrot' of verses 18–24, with the route to follow laid out in verses 12–17.

4 What's so terrible about God?

Joel 2:25–32

Verses 30–31 describe God's intervention in powerful and destructive language. The words are partly borrowed from descriptions of God's coming, such as in Exodus 19:18 (to Sinai) and Psalm 97 (to the temple), where also we find the theme of God destroying enemies. The other aspect is from descriptions of God's intervention in battle—the Day of the Lord. Altogether, this passage is an intensely frightening account of God's intervention, judgment and punishment (compare 2:1–11). Here the cosmic dimensions are heightened, too. But something has changed: the focus of the disturbance is no longer Israel or even the nations. Although the object of the divine energy is not specified, is it too much to see it as something beyond the human realm altogether—what the New Testament refers to as 'the powers' (for example, Colossians 1:16; 1 Peter 3:22)?

In any case, all the preceding verses are about amazing blessing and restoration, going beyond the losses previously endured. It includes abundance of physical provision (v. 26) but also spiritual provision, with the outpouring of God's Spirit on every category of people (vv. 28–29), emphasising both the abundance and the spread. These latter verses would form the prophetic core for Peter's speech on the Day of Pentecost (see Acts 2).

God's people will respond wholeheartedly in praise because they will discern that their prosperity is God's doing. It comes not from themselves or from other gods, whether local baals or the gods of the superpowers. They will know that God is with them and they will never again be humiliated—the real heart of the covenant promises, which their earlier behaviour has jeopardised. Significantly, then, they are addressed as 'my people...' (v. 26), God's covenant partners. The passage ends with another promise that God will save everyone who 'calls on his name' (v. 32, NRSV) or, as it is translated here, 'faithfully worships him'.

So, what the 'terrifying' verses (vv. 30–31) indicate is that God's restoration involves his own appearance, is costly and disrupts the normal order of the universe. Blessing does not come cheaply—to God. Perhaps we should see the unveiling of these verses in the incarnation and crucifixion of Jesus.

5 Judgment and justice

Joel 3:1–15

How does a civilised nation handle terrorists who are committed to the destruction of people and property and regard their own self-destruction as martyrdom and deliverance? The threat of execution is clearly no threat to them! While the death of a terrorist eliminates that one, experience tells us that it generates many more. Is torture justified in order to gain information to protect the people?

These kinds of questions remind us that it is no easy task to establish a peace that is sustainable and creates a context for development and creativity. We should not be too surprised, then, when the Old Testament often shows us the destruction of enemies as the complement to God's blessing his people with peace and prosperity. The prophetic books like Jeremiah and Ezekiel are structured in this way and so is the book of Joel.

We misunderstand 3:1–15, however, if we regard the passage merely as the overflow of Israel's revengeful attitude towards its neighbours. As in processes like South Africa's Truth and Reconciliation Commission, these verses are founded on the realisation that peace, justice and a wholesome society require the containment of evil, that is achieved partly by making justice clear to all.

The passage emphasizes that God is the establisher of justice, not that his people are to seek revenge against other nations. So the affront by Tyre, Sidon and Philistia is not against Israel but against God (see vv. 2, 5). Although the contest is depicted as a battle, God is judging the nations (v. 12), and there is even an apocalyptic emphasis (v. 15). In fact, these verses are applying the conditions of the covenant. To what extent they were understood as a description of reality and to what extent they were understood as metaphor, we can no longer determine, but the need for restraining justice as well as the gift of peace is the important message.

6 The lion roars: the sheep are safe!

Joel 3:16–21

As you are walking through the woods, a large dog rushes up to you, barking fiercely. Are you terrified or comforted? If it is an unknown dog and the owners are not in sight, probably fear is an appropriate reaction, for you do not know if it will attack you and there is no one to control it. On the other hand, if you are being threatened by other people and the dog is yours, it will bring relief and protection.

The presence of God is awesome—like the roar of a lion—especially when he comes to establish his kingdom (see Psalm 97, for instance). For God's people, however, this means that they are now safe: he is their fortress.

So the covenant is re-established: 'I am the Lord your God' (v. 17). Prosperity follows: the city is perpetually safe from invasion, both crops and animals flourish and there is no shortage of water. Indeed, as Ezekiel was to describe at much greater length (Ezekiel 47), water will flow from God's temple into the Dead Sea area (if the CEV is correct to interpret in this way). What is critical here is that the source of the fertility (water) flows from God (his temple).

Thus the horrors with which the prophecy began have been worked through—because of God's love and justice.

Guidelines
- Is there a role for the prophet today in the church and/or in society? Who might fulfil these roles? What might be the core messages?
- How important for us is the mixture of ritual and personal reality in our relationship to God (see Joel 2)? Can personal response ever be an adequate substitute for corporate involvement and practice? What are the dangers in each and how can they be mitigated? How do you balance them out in your own discipleship?
- How does God balance the need for justice with restoration in the New Testament? Is it seen differently for persons and nations? How might passages like Joel 3:1–15 help someone who has lived in a brutalising context, whether an oppressive nation such as Rwanda or Iraq, or an abusive home?

Pray for individuals and nations who are experiencing trauma, that through the terror they may discern the presence and deliverance of God.

The BRF

Magazine

Richard Fisher writes...

For Bible Sunday 2008 we started an initiative called 'The Bible Unwrapped: turn the page'. We offered packs containing sermon notes from David Winter, all-age sketches from the *Barnabas* team, two weeks of Bible readings and more, all to help promote Bible reading. This year, Bible Sunday is on 25 October, and, building on the popularity of the scheme in 2008, we are offering another pack (see the form on page 157 if you would like to order one).

Bible Sunday offers every church a valuable opportunity to encourage Bible reading within their congregation. Such an occasion can be just what is needed to focus attention on this vital aspect of our relationship with God.

Perhaps Bible Sunday will also inspire you to give a lasting gift this Christmas. Your church may appreciate a gift pack of Bible reading notes, Bibles for children or any of the other BRF and Barnabas resources on offer to equip them in their ministry.

Telling people in your church or further afield about your own experience with reading the Bible and how it has impacted on your life may also be a gift you could give. Sharing our stories with family, friends—even those we've just met over coffee after the service—can have a greater effect than we might realise.

In this issue of the BRF Magazine, Lisa Cherrett explains the new direction for *Guidelines* as from the next issue, Ceri Ellis discusses our Quiet Days and Events programme, Jane Butcher talks about building a foundation of faith at home and not just at church, Naomi Starkey previews some of our upcoming titles, and there's some exciting news of a major development with our discipleship resource *Foundations21*. There is also an extract from BRF's Advent book for 2009, *Shock and Awe* by Ian Coffey.

Richard Fisher
Chief Executive

Guidelines: the new look

Lisa Cherrett

As you're well aware, *Guidelines* holds a unique position as a series of notes that offers in-depth Bible study of a more scholarly nature than the usual devotional 'thought for the day'. For more than 20 years we have been aiming to provoke thought, nourish faith and broaden understanding of the scriptures through the expertise of biblical scholars from the academic world.

From the January–April 2010 issue onward, though, we want to develop *Guidelines* with a more practical, applied approach to theological study. While maintaining the scholarly standard of the writing, we plan to bring in a stronger focus on resourcing those who are meeting the demands of mission and disciple-building in today's church.

Every era brings new challenges to the church. In our own time, we see Christian faith being pushed to the edges rather than acknowledged as central to our culture—and churches are responding with new ways of expressing their witness within the communities they serve. There is a real need for Christian leaders in the church and secular society to be equipped to guide us into and through these unfamiliar waters, to wrestle with a wide range of practical discipleship issues and to promote a deep understanding of biblical doctrine in an anti-biblical climate.

Meeting the demands of mission and disciple-building in today's church

Those who do not see themselves as leaders, equally, may feel a more urgent desire to boost their confidence in explaining their faith to people whose knowledge of Christian teaching is minimal. They need the tools to think through faith issues for themselves rather than relying on other people's 'easy answers'. Whether we are a minister or lay person, then, each one of us needs to become, like Timothy, 'a worker who does not to need to be ashamed and who correctly han-

dles the word of truth' (2 Timothy 2:15, TNIV). We hope that *Guidelines* will play a major role in preparing its readers for these challenges.

For the past eight years, Dr Katharine Dell of the University of Cambridge has been responsible for commissioning studies on the Old Testament for *Guidelines*. This is Katharine's last issue as Editor, and we are most grateful to her for the work she has done in bringing the Old Testament alive for us for the last 24 issues. Many of the letters we've received from readers over the years have praised the fresh insights into Old Testament books that might seem dry and daunting at first sight—for example, Philip Jenson's notes on Leviticus in May–August 2005. We've benefited from Katharine's expertise as a contributor also, especially on the Wisdom writings, and we'd like to thank her and wish her well for the future.

As from January 2010, Canon Dr Jeremy Duff of Liverpool Cathedral, currently New Testament Editor, will become sole Commissioning Editor for *Guidelines*. This does not mean, of course, that we mean to neglect Old Testament study! We remain committed to the whole Bible as a source of inspiration and guidance for everyday life in the church and the world. We also intend to maintain a mixture of systematic study of individual Bible books and thematic study drawing on insights from several books across both Testaments. The Gospels will also continue to be covered in every issue. Strands encompassing mission and leadership, doctrine, church seasons, ethics and cultural issues, as well as prayer and spirituality, will all be woven in, not necessarily in every issue but regularly over the year.

The format of the notes, with weekly sections of six readings plus 'Guidelines', will stay the same, but the covers have been redesigned, using images that are more active, outward-looking and contemporary (see the inside front cover for examples). We hope that the fresh design will help us to reach new readers as well as continuing to engage the interest of those who have been loyal to *Guidelines* over many years.

The new year kicks off with studies on Luke, Isaiah, Malachi, the death of Jesus in John's Gospel, leadership, the Bible and politics, Old Testament theology and 'prayer in the busyness of life'. If you would be interested in receiving an extra, complementary copy of *Guidelines Jan–April 2010* to give to a friend or colleague, please phone the BRF office on 01865 319700, or email enquiries@brf.org.uk. We look forward to welcoming you to the new-look notes!

Lisa Cherrett is BRF's Project Editor and Managing Editor for the Bible reading notes.

A gift to the church

Richard Fisher

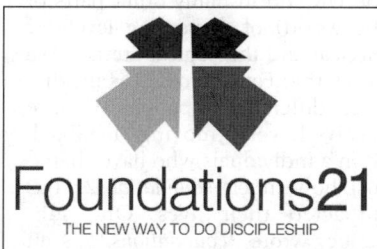

Foundations21
THE NEW WAY TO DO DISCIPLESHIP

Earlier this year we began to offer *Foundations21* free of charge, in place of the previous subscription-based approach. This has been a real step of faith, but it reflects our fundamental desire to make *Foundations21* accessible to as many people as possible, as a resource for lifelong Christian learning and discipleship.

We launched *Foundations21* back in July 2006. Since then, several hundred people have subscribed and more than 1000 people have taken various trial versions. However, although the response from everyone who has seen it has been that it's a remarkable resource, the prevailing view is that content on the web should be free.

Our motivation for developing *Foundations21*, and the motivation of those who so generously funded the project to its launch, was to develop a *new* way of doing discipleship, a *new* way to resource lifelong Christian learning for adults, an approach that embraced the multimedia opportunities offered by the web and was flexible enough to suit different lifestyles as well as different learning styles. No longer would one size have to fit all.

We wrestled for quite some time with the challenge of how to square our vision of making *Foundations21*

available as widely as possible with the need to be able to cover the annual overheads involved. Finally, towards the end of 2008, we took a deep breath and decided to offer *Foundations21* as a gift to the church—free of charge to anyone who wants to use it—and to seek the support of churches, trusts and individuals to secure the funding we need.

At the heart of BRF's ministry is a desire to equip people for Christian living. This involves three strands—helping people to read and understand the Bible, helping them to explore prayer and helping them to grow as disciples of Jesus Christ. *Foundations21* brings all three together.

Through *Foundations21* we want to make a difference and change lives; through *Foundations21* we believe that BRF can make a real contribution towards addressing the challenge in many churches (in the UK and in many other parts of the world) of decreasing levels of biblical and theological literacy. We know that *Foundations21* is making a real difference to people. We have received very moving feedback from a individuals who have shared just how much *Foundations21* has impacted their lives. One subscriber wrote, '*Foundations21* is an answer to prayer! It fits in so well with my family life and I can work through it at my own pace when it is convenient for me to do so.'

By removing the cost factor, we remove what we believe is a significant obstacle preventing the resource from being used more widely. It means we can redirect our energy from focusing on the question 'What is *Foundations21*?' and trying to persuade people to buy it, to asking 'How can you make best use of it?'

This opens up so many opportunities. We are talking to army chaplains, armed forces organisations, workplace ministry organisations, mission organisations, people involved with adult learning, people delivering lay training and continuing ministerial education programmes, vocations advisers, children's advisers and youth organisations. We are currently piloting the use of *Foundations21* in various contexts in three Anglican dioceses and we're talking to numerous other churches and groups. There is considerable interest in *Foundations21* as a resource for small groups, one-to-one mentoring, discipling new Christians, and connecting with those who are dispersed (for example, mission partners and those whose work patterns mean they can't be part of small group life in their church) and people who find it difficult to be part of conventional groups (for example, stroke victims and those with hearing difficulties). There is also interest in the potential for *Foundations21* to be of use within theological colleges in Africa and Asia.

We need to secure £65,000 a year to cover the costs of our *Foundations21* ministry and we're seeking funding support for this goal. We believe that support from churches and individuals will grow over time as they make use of *Foundations21* themselves and catch the vision for making it available to others.

Have you had a look at *Foundations21* yourself? Do you know people who might be interested in it? How about your church? Please help us spread the word about it, and let's get as many people as we can engaged in exploring and deepening their relationship with God and becoming even more effective disciples of Jesus Christ.

If you want to find out more or sign up for a copy yourself, you can do so by going to: www.foundations21.org.uk.

BRF's Quiet Days

Ceri Ellis

On an average working day, I will get up, go to work, come home, rush off for some kind of extra-curricular activity—a rehearsal for a concert, a church function, a meal out with friends—and go to bed again. In all the busyness of life, sometimes the only 'quiet time' I can find will be when I'm asleep!

I'm not the only one who has this experience of life: I hear the same story from friends, family, church members and co-workers. It's easy to fill every waking hour with this or that, and not have the chance to just sit, for five minutes or an hour or more, and rest.

BRF's Quiet Days have been running since the late 1990s, giving busy people the opportunity to step out of the race from dawn to dusk and listen to what God is saying. In the first half of 2009 alone, over 200 people have visited different venues around the country to take part in a Quiet Day. 2008 saw over 370 people come to rest in the Lord's presence under the guidance of our experienced speakers.

It has been my job, as Events Coordinator, to plan, book and organise all the Quiet Days since I took up the post in late 2007. The whole experience is enjoyable as I learn more about the events, the venues and the speakers, as well as sometimes getting the chance to meet the people who attend. Since I started, I have attended nine Quiet Days to assist speakers and take part as much as possible throughout the day.

The days usually follow a similar structure, with two sessions led by the speaker in the morning, then lunch and a further session. Each led session is followed by a period of quiet reflection, so the programme is carefully balanced to allow people to spend a significant portion of time listening to God's voice in the silence. Due to our varied list of speakers, including Simon Barrington-Ward, David Winter, Sister Helen Julian CSF and Jennifer Rees Larcombe, the led sessions are always thought-provoking and offer solid teaching on the subject of the day. Many days sell out, but the same level of calm and peace can be found on days with 35 people as on days with smaller numbers.

Each person attending a Quiet

Day will, of course, be affected differently, but I personally have found the days to be spiritually strengthening and an encouragement to my faith. It is surprisingly difficult to sit in quiet contemplation when you are not used to it, but sometimes that is the best way to truly hear what God is saying to us.

Jennifer Rees Larcombe is the author of *Beauty from Ashes* (BRF, 2000) and founder of a charity of the same name, which helps people whose lives have been distorted or broken by loss and trauma. Jennifer has been leading Quiet Days for BRF for many years. She says of the experience:

What always amazes me about Quiet Days is the way they seem to transform the way people look. So often they arrive worn down by life, drained of energy, looking white and strained—just as if they were in need of a good holiday. But when they leave at the end of the day, they look relaxed, rested and radiant—in fact, exactly as if they were returning from their two weeks' annual leave.

The programme for the rest of 2009 features some familiar faces and some new ones. Anne Hibbert is leading a day near Coventry on Proverbs; Maggi Dawn will be drawing on themes from her book *Beginnings and Endings (and what happens in between)* (BRF, 2007) at a day in Cambridgeshire; Ann Persson is speaking on the theme 'Invitation' near Henley-on-Thames in Oxfordshire. With Quiet Days and events stretching from September to December, there are many different themes and venues to choose from.

We also offer advice for people wishing to run Quiet Days of their own in their local area. We can advertise days like these on our website and through the special Quiet Days emailing list, which currently goes out to around 300 people. Through the Quiet Spaces website, you can find a set of guidelines on how to organise your own Quiet Day, covering everything from finding a speaker to arranging catering for the day. So if there isn't a BRF Quiet Day happening near you, why not consider hosting one of your own? Visit www.quietspaces.org.uk for more details, or contact the office on 01865 319700.

Our Quiet Day programme for 2009 is available in print from BRF. To request a print copy or to book a place on a Quiet Day, call 01865 319700 or write to the usual BRF address. You can also view the programme and book places online at www.quietspaces.org.uk/events.

Ceri Ellis is BRF's Events and Direct Marketing Coordinator. In her spare time, she enjoys writing novels, reading novels and singing.

Barnabas in Churches: what, how, when, why?

Jane Butcher

The heart of Barnabas in Churches is captured in the tagline 'Resourcing children's work in churches'. The form that takes can vary: it can involve direct contact with a church, either leading or working alongside a church team to run events such as *The Christmas Journey* or holiday Bible clubs, or running training events for an individual or group of churches. It can also entail leading sessions at Diocesan or ecumenical events that offer training and support for those involved in children's ministry.

Even when the *Barnabas* team cannot meet children's leaders face to face, we can offer other resources. There is a wealth of free, downloadable ideas on our website www.barnabasinchurches.org.uk and, of course, Barnabas publishes a range of written resources to assist children's ministry.

However, we are increasingly aware of the need to think outside the box regarding what 'church' looks like in today's society. Much research confirms the idea that Sunday, for many people, has changed in its style, and church is no longer part of the picture. This raises the question of whether there is a need to consider 'church outside Sunday' or 'midweek church'—a concept that is highlighted by the work of Fresh Expressions (see the website www.freshexpressions.org.uk). Messy Church is one example of a Fresh Expression of church, developed by Lucy Moore, a member of the *Barnabas* team. To find out more, do take a look at the website www.messychurch.org.uk.

But is faith development the role of the church alone (or, more particularly, the church and Sunday school leaders)? Maybe we need to look to the African proverb, 'It takes a village to raise a child.' If we transfer this idea to church, perhaps it indicates that the wider church has a role in nurturing children. It highlights the richness of relationships that can exist among people of all ages, genders and backgrounds. Are there church members who have experiences and abilities they could share with others? For example, could those with knitting, crochet or other craft skills visit the toddler or preschool groups to teach others? Are there people—teenagers or adults—with musical ability who could offer to do some singing at children's groups? These and many other possibilities allow shared experiences to enhance our relationships and our sense of belonging to the church family of which we are a part.

In addition, the *Barnabas* team has been considering how faith development can take place in the home—how all members of a family can experience and develop in their faith together. The church has been so long accustomed to being the focal point, as far as teaching and learning is concerned, that it really is hard to get out of that mindset, and we may rarely hear 'faith in the home' preached about. However, various pieces of research have confirmed that children are most influenced by their parent(s) or carer(s) and that the home is a significant place of learning.

This being the case, it suggests that home can offer an environment in which to enhance the development of faith. For many adults, however, this may raise some 'how' questions. How do you pray with children? How do you tell Bible stories with words that children can understand? How can we do activities that involve children of various ages?

One response would be to highlight the wealth of ideas that are now freely available on websites and in books and Bibles written specifically for children. In particular, there are many ways in which festivals and the everyday things of life can be used to help focus the thoughts of all family members and stimulate discussion.

For example, why not make a 'family favourites picture collage', allowing each person to contribute photographs, postcards or other items that remind them of a favourite time—maybe from the summer holidays or Christmas, or events in the last academic or calendar year. The collage can then be used as a springboard into prayer. Each day, possibly at breakfast or after an evening meal together, a different person could take a turn to point out their item, explain why it is special and thank God for that time.

There are many other activities that can draw on the everyday experiences of life to enhance the development of faith in people of all ages. What is important is for children and adults alike to experience significant opportunities that allow us all to draw closer to God and allow him to draw near to us.

Jane Butcher is a member of the Barnabas *team, based in the Midlands.*

The Editor recommends

Naomi Starkey

As the Bible Reading Fellowship, it is (to state the obvious) central to everything we do that we encourage people to read the Bible, to understand what they are reading, and to see how they can apply it to their lives. Reading the Bible, though, is not like reading any other book. Not only is it longer than most books (and the paper thinner and the print smaller) but, as we continue as Christian disciples, we find ourselves reading and rereading the same passages. It can be hard to carry on seeking new insights from a particular set of verses when we feel we know them inside out and back to front.

Over-familiarity can be a problem for preachers, too, particularly at Easter and Christmas, when the season demands the same sermon topic every year. Of course we can pray for the inspiration of the Holy Spirit, but we may still find it a real struggle to come up with an inspiring message, especially if the congregation is more or less still the same (and will eventually have heard all our best anecdotes and illustrations!).

Much of our publishing at BRF—both books and Bible reading notes—is geared to helping people reencounter familiar texts. It's not that the meaning itself has changed, but there may be unexpected connections, helpful applications and imaginative ways of accessing the original power of the passages. *The Real Godsend* by Dr

Nigel G. Wright is subtitled 'Preaching the birth narratives in Matthew and Luke', which sums up the book's aim: bringing out the powerful witness of what are probably the most familiar of all Bible passages.

The accounts of Jesus' birth tend to be seen as 'Christmas stories', overlaid with seasonal trimmings that, as often as not, stifle rather than clarify their meaning. *The Real Godsend* shows how we can preach and teach these well-known and well-loved narratives, revealing them as carefully crafted works of theology, written in the light of the resurrection and drawing on the Hebrew scriptures (the Old Testament) to reveal the nature of the God who sent his Son into the world.

At the same time, Nigel Wright

shows how these accounts do not simply relate ancient history but invite us to believe in the risen Christ who is alive now, the real Godsend who comes to us as God's greatest gift. Understanding the narratives at a deeper level means that we can use their vivid imagery and richly textured themes to communicate these most profound of truths.

In writing this book, Nigel Wright draws on a wealth of academic and pastoral experience. He is Principal of Spurgeon's College, London, a former president of the Baptist Union of Great Britain, and has also worked in two churches in the north of England. He has written extensively on issues of church renewal and has also written *God on the Inside: the Holy Spirit in Holy Scripture* for BRF.

While the Old Testament is less well-known, in general, than the New, one story that remains a perennial favourite is David and Goliath. The idea of the 'little man' who, despite inadequate weaponry, manages to kill the 'giant' is part of popular culture, as well as being reflected in this story in scripture, but too often it ends up being seen as more suitable for Sunday school material than as a topic for mature reflection. In *Confidence in the Living God*, Bishop Andrew Watson revisits the David and Goliath episode, using a narrative theology approach to reveal an underlying theme of confidence.

Confidence lies at the heart of our society, determining the success or failure of the economy, the government, companies, schools and churches. It also profoundly affects individual lives, whether we are members of a sports team, part of a business consortium or facing a major exam. As Christians, we are called to proclaim our faith in the living God, but how can we build this confidence in a culture where such faith is often dismissed as embarrassing or even downright dangerous?

Working systematically through the events of the Bible story as they unfold, Bishop Andrew not only provides useful background on the characters and historical context, but also shows how confidence is a central theme—and how it relates to our lives today. He reflects on God's ability to develop a proper self-confidence within individuals and his Church, so as to reveal the gospel through transforming words and transformed lives.

Confidence in the Living God is Bishop Andrew's second book for BRF, following *The Fourfold Leadership of Jesus* (2008). As Bishop of Aston he is involved in promoting church growth and leadership across the diocese of Birmingham. He was previously vicar of St Stephen's, East Twickenham, where he helped pioneer three church plants.

To order a copy of any of these books, please turn to the order form on page 159.

A extract from
Shock and Awe

In BRF's Advent book for 2009, author Ian Coffey explores our amazing, all-loving, all-powerful God and how he reaches out to save us—if we only put our trust in him. Starting with Abraham and concluding with the heavenly vision of Revelation, *Shock and Awe* reflects on some of the gifts that grace brings and shows what it means practically to live as followers of Christ and as people of hope. The following extract is an abridged version of the Introduction and the first day's reading.

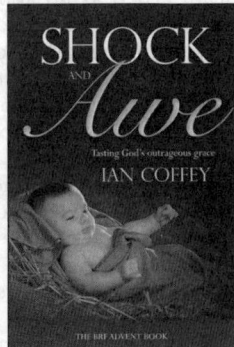

Introduction

Advent is a season of surprise.

The Bible readings and meditations in this book will regularly remind us that the incarnation of Jesus Christ, God's Son, was met with incredulity, wonder and astonishment... When I began to think about these Advent readings and how we might rediscover the wonder of the incarnation, I was gripped by a phrase that wouldn't let go of me: 'shock and awe'.

Mention the words 'shock and awe' to many people and they are instantly connected with the contentious military campaign launched against Iraq in 2003. But the phrase itself was borrowed by military commanders from a strategy developed some years previously at the National Defense University of the United States of America.

Two military strategists observed a lesson from history, stretching back many centuries: put simply, if you can overwhelm your enemy with an early strike of decisive force, then their will to resist is broken. By the process of shock, your opponent is awed into submission.

Leaving aside the controversy surrounding the decision to invade Iraq (a valid and important discussion for another place), I was struck by the description 'shock and awe' and the tacit assumption that this could only be achieved by bombs, bullets, might and power.

The kingdom of God is about shock and awe, but of a wholly different kind. The gospel of the Lord Jesus Christ is of a king who stoops to conquer, who washes the feet of his followers, takes the place of a lowly slave and is willing to pay the ultimate price of redeeming love through an ignominious and unjust death. There is no apparent might or power in a baby in a manger, or a man riding on a donkey surrounded by cheering children, or one nailed to a cross before a jeering crowd. But the important word here is 'apparent'.

The shock of the incarnation of the servant-king has led to a different kind of awe—not that of the subjugated, terrorised and submissive, but rather the awe of wonder, incredulity and love. Isaac Watts (1674–1748) had it right when he wrote that nothing in the whole of creation could respond to such amazing love without the giving of its whole self to God in grateful submission and service…

The big story of the Bible speaks of God's great rescue project for lost people. The theme of the story is grace (undeserved love) and his method, shock and awe. This is a God of surprises who chooses unlikely people and works in unusual ways. Our studies through this season of Advent will help us dip into that story and see firsthand what it involves.

We begin with Abram in the first book of the Bible, Genesis, and we conclude with a vision of God's future plan in the final book of Revelation. In between, we shall consider what it means to be people of faith, trusting God's promises and encountering him in new ways in our daily lives. We shall consider some of the gifts that grace brings and think about what it means practically to live as followers of Christ and as people of hope. It's my hope that this will be a positive learning experience as the Spirit of God impresses and underlines truth for us. I am reminded of Mohandas Gandhi's advice: 'Live as if you were to die tomorrow. Learn as if you were to live for ever'.

The studies have been prepared on the basis of daily readings over the six weeks of Advent, but a study guide has been included for those who may wish to compare notes with a wider group.

My prayer is that these studies will give us a deeper glimpse of what it means to taste outrageous grace and to live in the good of it… Let's explore this outrageous grace.

1 December: Faith that walks

READ GENESIS 12:1–5

My wife and I lived abroad for several years. I remember the work involved in moving—finding the best removal company, organising a house to rent, opening bank accounts, locating doctors and dentists, insuring the car—and all in a foreign language. We are glad we did it as the experience brought many good things—not least the capacity to empathise with anyone who announces, 'I am moving to work abroad.'

Abram faced a much bigger challenge. God asked him to set out for an unknown destination. His family had lived in the city of Ur (11:31), located in the region we know as southern Iraq. God had begun to speak to Abram and told him to leave everything familiar and secure and set out for somewhere better, yet to be revealed.

Abram and his family settled for a time in a place called Haran, a bustling caravan city. The Bible doesn't tell us why he took the decision to stay there: it may have been due to circumstances beyond his control. During this time, his father Terah died and Abram and his entourage then journeyed on towards the land of Canaan. This sets the scene for the remarkable promise that God gave to Abram—a promise that has implications for us as well.

It is not clear from Genesis when the promise was made—it could date back to the time when he was living in Ur—but the details are very clear. The promise is made up of seven strands set out in our reading.

- From Abram will come a great nation.
- Abram will be blessed by God.
- Abram's name will be made great.
- He will be a blessing.
- Those who bless him (treat him well) will be blessed by God.
- Those who curse him (treat him badly) will be cursed by God.
- All peoples on earth will be blessed through Abram.

I can't begin to imagine the impact this news must have had on Abram. My mind is filled with questions.

How did he know that this was God speaking and not his overactive imagination? Did he tell his wife and family about the promise? Did he have doubts on the journey? What did his friends in Ur and Haran say about the move?

The Bible doesn't answer my questions but leaves me with this faith-filled phrase: 'So Abram left, as the Lord had told him' (v. 4). That's all I need to know. Abram's faith led to obedient action, and that meant taking a long walk to a new place that God would show him at some future date.

We sometimes make the mistake of thinking that everything needs to be mapped out and planned before we take the step of faith. If that were so, then faith would not be necessary as the path ahead would be obvious. Faith means trusting God when sometimes all we can see is the next step. As we take that step, we trust that the next one will become visible.

Is there a step of faith and obedience that you need to take? Let Abram's example inspire you.

Reflect

'We live by faith, not by sight' (2 Corinthians 5:7).

Father God, teach me to walk by faith, trusting completely in your fatherly care. Amen

To order a copy of this book, please turn to the order form on page 159.

Guidelines © BRF 2009

The Bible Reading Fellowship
15 The Chambers, Vineyard, Abingdon OX14 3FE, United Kingdom
Tel: 01865 319700; Fax: 01865 319701
E-mail: enquiries@brf.org.uk
Website: www.brf.org.uk

ISBN 978 1 84101 523 1

Distributed in Australia by:
Willow Connection, PO Box 288, Brookvale, NSW 2100.
Tel: 02 9948 3957; Fax: 02 9948 8153;
E-mail: info@willowconnection.com.au
Available also from all good Christian bookshops in Australia.
For individual and group subscriptions in Australia:
Mrs Rosemary Morrall, PO Box W35, Wanniassa, ACT 2903.

Distributed in New Zealand by:
Scripture Union Wholesale, PO Box 760, Wellington
Tel: 04 385 0421; Fax: 04 384 3990; E-mail: suwholesale@clear.net.nz

Distributed in Canada by:
The Anglican Book Centre, 80 Hayden Street, Toronto, Ontario, M4Y 3G2
Tel: 001 416 924-1332; Fax: 001 416 924-2760;
E-mail: abc@anglicanbookcentre.com; Website: www.anglicanbookcentre.com

Publications distributed to more than 60 countries

Printed in Singapore by Craft Print International Ltd

SUPPORTING BRF'S MINISTRY

As a Christian charity, BRF is involved in five distinct yet complementary areas. Through our **BRF** ministry (www.brf.org.uk), we're resourcing adults for their spiritual journey through Bible reading notes, books, and a programme of quiet days and teaching days. BRF also provides the infrastructure that supports our other four specialist ministries.

Our **Foundations21** ministry (www.foundations21.org.uk) is providing flexible and innovative ways for individuals and groups to explore their Christian faith and discipleship through a multimedia internet-based resource.

Led by Lucy Moore, our **Messy Church** ministry is enabling churches all over the UK (and increasingly abroad) to reach children and adults beyond the fringes of the church (visit www.messychurch.org.uk).

Through our **Barnabas in Churches** ministry, we're helping churches to support, resource and develop their children's ministry with the under-11s more effectively (visit www.barnabasinchurches.org.uk).

Our **Barnabas in Schools** ministry (www.barnabasinschools.org.uk) is enabling primary school children and teachers to explore Christianity creatively and bring the Bible alive within RE and Collective Worship.

At the heart of BRF's ministry is a desire to equip adults and children for Christian living—helping them to read and understand the Bible, to explore prayer and to grow as disciples of Jesus. In an increasingly secular world, people need this help more than ever. We can do something about it, but our resources are limited. We need your help to make a real impact on the local church, local schools and the wider community.

- You could support BRF's ministry with a donation or standing order (using the response form overleaf).
- You could consider making a bequest to BRF in your will. (We have a leaflet available with more information about this, which can be requested using the form overleaf.)
- You could encourage your church to support BRF as part of your church's giving to home mission—perhaps focusing on a specific area of our ministry, or a particular member of our *Barnabas* team.
- Most important of all, you could support BRF with your prayers.

If you would like to discuss how a specific gift or bequest could be used in the development of our ministry, Chief Executive Richard Fisher would be delighted to talk further with you, either on the telephone or in person. Please let us know if you would like him to contact you.

Whatever you can do or give, we thank you for your support.

BRF MINISTRY APPEAL RESPONSE FORM

Name _____

Address _____

_____ Postcode _____

Telephone _____ Email _____

(tick as appropriate)

Gift Aid Declaration

☐ I am a UK taxpayer. I want BRF to treat as Gift Aid Donations all donations I make from 6 April 2000 until I notify you otherwise.

Signature _____ Date _____

☐ I would like to support BRF's ministry with a regular donation by standing order (please complete the Banker's Order below).

Standing Order – Banker's Order

To the Manager, Name of Bank/Building Society _____

Address _____

_____ Postcode _____

Sort Code _____ Account Name _____

Account No _____

Please pay Royal Bank of Scotland plc, Drummonds, 49 Charing Cross, London SW1A 2DX (Sort Code 16-00-38), for the account of BRF A/C No. 00774151

The sum of _____ pounds on ___ / ___ / ___ (insert date your standing order starts) and thereafter the same amount on the same day of each month until further notice.

Signature _____ Date _____

Single donation

☐ I enclose my cheque/credit card/Switch card details for a donation of

£5 £10 £25 £50 £100 £250 (other) £ _____ to support BRF's ministry

Credit/Switch card no. ☐☐☐☐☐☐☐☐☐☐☐☐☐☐☐☐☐☐☐☐

Expires ☐☐☐☐ Security code ☐☐☐ Issue no. of Switch card ☐☐☐☐

Signature _____ Date _____

(Where appropriate, on receipt of your donation, we will send you a Gift Aid form)

☐ Please send me information about making a bequest to BRF in my will.

Please detach and send this completed form to: Richard Fisher, BRF, 15 The Chambers, Vineyard, Abingdon OX14 3FE. BRF is a Registered Charity (No.233280)

BIBLE READING RESOURCES PACK

An updated pack of resources and ideas to help to promote Bible reading in your church is available from BRF. The pack, which will be of use at any time during the year (but especially for Bible Sunday in October), includes sample readings from BRF's Bible reading notes and *The People's Bible Commentary*, a sermon outline, an all-age sketch, a children's activity, information about BRF's ministry and much more.

Unless you specify the month in which you would like the pack sent, we will send it immediately on receipt of your order. We greatly appreciate your donations towards the cost of producing the pack (without them we would not be able to make the pack available) and we welcome your comments about the contents of the pack and your ideas for future ones.

This coupon should be sent to:

BRF
15 The Chambers
Vineyard
Abingdon
OX14 3FE

Name ————————————————————————

Address ————————————————————————

————————————————————————————————

——————————————————————— Postcode ——————

Telephone ——————————————————————

Email ————————————————————————————

Please send me ——— Bible Reading Resources Pack(s)

Please send the pack now/ in ———————————(month).

I enclose a donation for £ ——— towards the cost of the pack.

BRF is a Registered Charity

❏ Please send me a Bible reading resources pack
❏ I would like to take out a subscription myself (complete your name and address details only once)
❏ I would like to give a gift subscription (please complete both name and address sections below)

Your name _____

Your address _____

_____Postcode _____

Gift subscription name _____

Gift subscription address _____

_____Postcode _____

Gift message (20 words max.) _____

_____

Please send *Guidelines* beginning with the January / May / September 2010 issue: (delete as applicable)

(please tick box)	UK	SURFACE	AIR MAIL
GUIDELINES	❏ £13.80	❏ £15.00	❏ £17.10
GUIDELINES 3-year sub	❏ £33.00		
GUIDELINES with *New Daylight* by daily email	❏ £21.60		

Your email address _____

Please complete the payment details below and send, with appropriate payment, to: **BRF, 15 The Chambers, Vineyard, Abingdon OX14 3FE.**

Total enclosed £ _____ (cheques should be made payable to 'BRF')

Payment by cheque ❏ postal order ❏ Visa ❏ Mastercard ❏ Switch ❏

Card number: ⬚⬚⬚⬚⬚⬚⬚⬚⬚⬚⬚⬚⬚⬚⬚⬚⬚⬚

Expires: ⬚⬚⬚⬚   Security code ⬚⬚⬚   Issue no (Switch): ⬚⬚⬚⬚

Signature (essential if paying by credit/Switch) ——————————————

Please ensure that you complete and send off both sides of this order form.

Please send me the following book(s):

		Quantity	Price	Total
Books for Advent and Christmas:				
641 2	Shock and Awe (*I. Coffey*)	_____	£6.99	_____
247 6	A Handful of Light (*M. Mitton*)	_____	£7.99	_____
566 8	Beginnings and Endings (*M. Dawn*)	_____	£7.99	_____
677 1	Five Impossible Things to Believe before Christmas (*K. Scully*)	_____	£5.99	_____
705 1	Silent Night (*V. Howie*)	_____	£7.99	_____
585 9	Easy Ways to Christmas Plays 2 (*V. Howie*)	_____	£11.99	_____
623 8	Looking Forward to Christmas with Timothy Bear (*B. Sears*)	_____	£7.99	_____
684 9	Christmas Sticker Collection (*S. Box*)	_____	£3.99	_____
621 4	The Christmas Journey (*M. Curry & G. Morgan*)	_____	£6.99	_____
Recommended books/authors in this issue				
576 7	The Real Godsend (*N. Wright*)	_____	£7.99	_____
484 5	God on the Inside (*N. Wright*)	_____	£7.99	_____
643 6	Confidence in the Living God (*A. Watson*)	_____	£7.99	_____
435 7	The Fourfold Leadership of Jesus (*A. Watson*)	_____	£7.99	_____
030 4	PBC: 1 & 2 Samuel (*H. Mowvley*)	_____	£7.99	_____
118 9	PBC: 1 & 2 Kings (*S.B. Dawes*)	_____	£7.99	_____
245 2	PBC: Hosea to Micah (*P. Gooder*)	_____	£8.99	_____
046 5	PBC: Mark (*D. France*)	_____	£8.99	_____

Total cost of books £ _____

Donation £ _____

Postage and packing £ _____

TOTAL £ _____

POSTAGE AND PACKING CHARGES				
order value	UK	Europe	Surface	Air Mail
£7.00 & under	£1.25	£3.00	£3.50	£5.50
£7.01–£30.00	£2.25	£5.50	£6.50	£10.00
Over £30.00	free	prices on request		

See over for payment details. All prices are correct at time of going to press, are subject to the prevailing rate of VAT and may be subject to change without prior warning.

PAYMENT DETAILS

Please complete the payment details below and send with appropriate payment and completed order form to:

**BRF, 15 The Chambers, Vineyard,
Abingdon OX14 3FE**

Name _____

Address _____

_____ Postcode _____

Telephone _____

Email _____

Total enclosed £ _____(cheques should be made payable to 'BRF')

Payment by cheque ❏ postal order ❏ Visa ❏ Mastercard ❏ Switch ❏

Card number: ☐☐☐☐☐☐☐☐☐☐☐☐☐☐☐☐☐☐☐

Expires: ☐☐☐☐ Security code ☐☐☐ Issue no (Switch): ☐☐☐

Signature (essential if paying by credit/Switch card)_____

❏ Please do not send me further information about BRF publications.

ALTERNATIVE WAYS TO ORDER

Christian bookshops: All good Christian bookshops stock BRF publications. For your nearest stockist, please contact BRF.

Telephone: The BRF office is open between 09.15 and 17.30.
To place your order, phone 01865 319700; fax 01865 319701.

Web: Visit www.brf.org.uk

GL0309